THE SINGING WARRIOR

A WOMAN'S STRUGGLE
TO EMPOWER HERSELF
DESPITE HER ABUSIVE PAST

Published in 2010 by Summertime Publishing

Text copyright © Niamh Ni Bhroin

ISBN 978-1-904881-31-5

Design and layout by www.creationbooth.com

Printed in the United Kingdom
Summertime Publishing
www.summertimepublishing.com

The events that take place in this book are true, however some names and details have been changed to protect the identities of those involved.

Acknowledgements

On my journey from Ireland to England, Greece and the Netherlands - the country does not matter if you are always running away from yourself.

Thanks to

Emer O'Broin-McCauley, shamanic practitioner,
who showed me the way
Thomas Grufferty, shaman,
who would not leave me behind
Eileen Tobin, shamanic practitioner,
who gave me her gentle powerful strength
My Healing Group in Scotland, Aberdeen (26th March, 2010),
who shared my pain and struggles
Toirdhealbhach O'Broin, my brother,
who believed in me
Eoghan O'Broin, my brother,
who was just always there for me
Oisin, our daughter,
who always accepted me as I am,
she is destined to journey on a path of love and light
All the friends I have lost along the way
All the friends I have found on this magical new endeavour
My departed mother who did the best she could. I never stopped loving her
My departed father who made me the warrior that I am today
My ex-husband,
without our pain, I could not have found my true path

My editor Jo Parfitt,
who only encouraged and inspired me
Billy Allwood and Holly Marder, editors,
who gave me loads of opportunities to write articles for
their publications
Therese Coyne,
who never doubted me
Helen Freney,
who gave me her friendship
Bernie Larkin,
who was always kind
Mary Gavin,
who was just there for me
Annette Letsch,
who gave me her sisterly advice and love
Maria Piscopo,
who always listened to me
The Irish Club, the Hague
ACCESS, voluntary organization for ex-pats, the Hague
Casa Di Bella, Rocco and Bertine,
their little café was always my sanctuary and all the
friends I met there
La Buena Vida, Paul and Ginny,
who always made me feel welcome
Peter Hoogsteden,
for being such a great friend and musical partner
Christine Fischer and Bram Visser,
for their unconditional support

A special thanks to my canine friend Mozart,
who never left my side whilst I was writing this book.

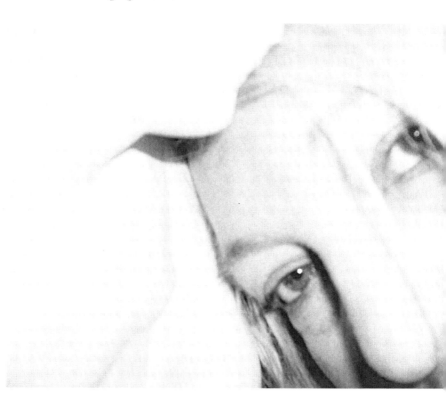

About the author

Niamh Ni Bhroin is currently living in the Hague, the Netherlands with her daughter. She is finding herself through her writing and warrior's journey while trying to break through as a full-time writer. Niamh regularly gives readings to women who have been in similar abusive situations. She writes a weekly column, called Cloggy Valley, for www.thehagueonline.com and recently set up a company called Celtic Warrior. Her main goal is to give singing and writing workshops and share her experiences with others. Her love of children's theatre has never left her and her 'Flying Trapeze' children's puppet shows are well-known in the area where she lives.

The Singing Warrior

Preface

The Masai warrior stood tall and his ochre-painted face glowed a deep orange in the African midday sun. His beauty was flawed by a very large ragged scar that ran down his left forearm. I was fascinated by it and approached him when my safari group started to scatter in front of me. Oisin and her father had joined the rest of the tourists and I was compelled to wait for our colourful bodyguard.

"How did you get such a scar on your arm? Did you have an accident?" I asked.

"No, Big Mama, I fought a lion," he replied. "I begged him to spare my life and he left me with a reminder of his great power. My life was in his hands and he chose to give it back to me. Such greatness is part of our journey in life."

I looked at him and felt an unspoken message in his words. He suddenly took my two hands and clasped them in his long fingers. It was such an unexpected movement that I had no time to react. We stood there and he continued. I felt his cool hands on my sweaty palms.

"Big Mama, your journey has not yet taken place. You will have to face your greatness with much pain but a new life will await you. You cannot go back to the old life. Big Mama knows that."

I broke away from our entwined fingers and ran towards the rest of the group, desperately and breathlessly. Oisin ran up to greet me. I embraced her and couldn't let her go. She escaped my arms and her father looked at me curiously. I knew that things were changing. Little did I know that four months later, my life would be transformed forever.

The Singing Warrior

CHAPTER 1

FIFTY
FAT, FREE, FLAT BROKE

I sat there with my eleven-year-old daughter, Oisin, and took stock of our new furnished apartment. It was light and airy and I had to climb up two flights of grey, slightly greasy, concrete steps to reach the scratched front door. I was not sure if I loved it or hated it. Turlough and Eoghan stood there, trying to look comfortable. Turlough, tall and tanned, blue checkered shirt open at the neck. He was stroking his Viking beard and pacing up and down. This was Turlough's way of relaxing. He gave me one of his mischievous grins. His silver tooth made him look like a pirate. I longed for him to give me one of his famous bear hugs and to take Oisin and me away from everything. He had sailed around the world when he was a young man. I imagined us all on this giant sailing boat and I heard myself growling: "Aye, Aye Captain, land ahead." He had had a very adventurous life. Turlough had flown over from his home in Scotland to help us. He had just returned from offshore in Dubai and boomed out instructions. He was deaf in one ear from all his years as a deepsea diver. Oisin and I loved his deep baritone voice. It filled the emptiness.

"Uncle Turlough you're so funny. Tell me your stories again," Oisin giggled.

But for now, he was serious. He looked at me with his glistening blue eyes. I knew he was trying to be strong for all of us.

"Eoghan and I will go out and get some shopping. Oisin, you can take Mozart for a walk . . ."

"Are you happy, Niamh?" Eoghan asked, gesturing towards the cheaply renovated apartment. His eyes scanned the balding brown carpet, the do-it-yourself double glazing and the rough stucco walls that would scratch my forehead when I lent against them and cried later that day. He sat down on the grubby beige settee and for a minute I was afraid that it would collapse under his weight. Years of medication had taken its toll on my second brother. His pale, bloated face was such a contrast to his elder brother. He nervously began to roll a cigarette. His nicotine-stained fingers moved slowly and methodically. I didn't have the heart to tell him to smoke outside. Eoghan's life had been another sort of adventure. He had given up on life, whilst his older brother lived it to the fullest. Where was I then, in this? Was I in the middle – a combination of giving up and hanging on to life itself? A picture of the three of us as children flickered through my memory. One tall, skinny boy, flirting with the camera, one smaller, stockier boy shying away from it and one white-blonde girl unsure of what she should do, just standing there.

"Yes," I replied. "Yes I am." I smiled broadly. I had left my marriage after eighteen years. I was a single mother in a foreign country. I wouldn't burden my brothers with my turmoil. I sat down beside him and held his puffy hand. It trembled and I patted it in a motherly fashion. I felt such empathy with Eoghan but I had to keep focused. It would be better if he left with Turlough. Turlough was staying with him for a few days. I knew he loved being with his outgoing brother and it was time for me to be on my own.

Eoghan and Turlough said their goodbyes and Oisin took Mozart out for a walk along the pavements, past the shops beneath our second floor apartment to the scrape of grass on the corner. I'd bought the black and white mongrel with the velvet ears for us both to compensate for wrenching us from our comfortable detached house and her father. Mozart was a mix of everything, like my life. One big bloody mess. His long body was hoisted onto short little legs, defying gravity. I sometimes wondered if his heart wasn't a little too far from the rest of him. My own heart seemed to have stopped beating a long time ago. I pressed my flattened palm to my breastbone and sighed with relief. There was something pulsing away in there, at least, but I did not recognise its beat.

The sun shone in through the window, intruding on my despair. I had now one hundred euros in my purse. Mozart had been an impulse purchase. Typical me, I didn't think of the greater picture. But I had no regrets. Mozart was a great distraction for Oisin. Somehow, I knew that he would be a bigger distraction for me. I would have to get up in the morning to let him out to pee. No excuse to pull the covers over my head and burrow back into the warmth and sleep. Turlough had paid three months rent in advance for me. Three months before reality would strike.

"Mom, if we were to live in a tent, I would go with you," Oisin had said.

What if we did end up living in the Westbroekpark under the chestnut trees beside the lake? I pictured us in a huge Bedouin tent surrounded by the dazzling colours of the desert. We could light candles at night and snuggle together in the lightweight sleeping bags we had hastily packed along with the rest of our sparse luggage. I looked at the two yellow IKEA bags and my daughter's violin. They represented my twenty years in Holland and Oisin's eleven. That was it. That was us. That was the price we paid for making a quick exit.

I tried to make sense of things but a black cloud of despair fell around my shoulders. How I had ended up here, in The Hague, at fifty years old was a mystery, the reasons and the chance occurrences buried in a murky mist of hazy recollections.

I remembered leaving him a note.

"I came to Holland 20 years ago with 200 guilders, I am leaving now with 200 euros. Ain't life funny eh?"

I didn't think Lucas would get the joke. The shit would hit the fan soon enough. What is it he used to say? "Don't get mad, get even." Does that apply to me too? A clammy sweat broke out over my whole body. Is this the way to handle things? So many questions, so few answers. I froze thinking of the hurt I'd caused. It was too painful to think about. Love wasn't meant to cause such heartache.

With Eoghan, Turlough and Oisin out of the way, I kicked off my black leather boots, stepped into the shower, fully clothed, and howled. I howled like a wounded animal, the cries reverberating on the sky-blue walls. I concentrated on a chip on one of the tiles. Another example of shoddy workmanship. My bare feet tried to find some solace on the cold tiles of the raised shower floor.

My toes clung to the raw ledge as if to stop me from going over some precipice. The warm water dripped down my trouser legs and I watched, mesmerised, as the black dye mingled with the wetness. I found it soothing. It reminded me of the black inkwell on my first day at school. The dark whirlpool had invited me in. The grey-black water gurgled down the plughole. It stalled and gurgled again. When it had disappeared, I stepped out. My footsteps followed me and I circled around, like a caged animal, to confuse them.

I had stopped asking for someone to listen. My howling came from a dark place, low in my belly. The apartment terrified me. Its ceilings were too high. The windows too wide and the walls too white. There were no dark wardrobes to loom lugubriously at me from the walls. I had no possessions to tidy away anyway and I was grateful. I walked around in more damp circles. For once in my life this had been my choice, my doing. I had chosen this prison for myself.

I stripped off my wet clothes and stood there naked. I saw the reflection of my middle-aged body in a tall mirror. An overweight middle-aged body. It disgusted me and I turned away. I could see that I was no longer a little girl. My long white blonde hair dripped fat tears onto the worn patterned carpet of my new bedroom. The colours seem to brighten with each splash. I shook myself and tried to pull myself together.. I had escaped. I should feel glad. But had I really escaped? Had I not just run away from myself? Different place, same me. I knew I could not go back. My marriage was over. I had to move on to wherever life took me. I felt nauseous, empty.

The kitchen drawer was filled with knives and I could feel them beckoning. Their steely loveliness whispered to me through the cheap imitation wooden drawers. They winked at me and laughed.

"Go to hell, all of you!" I screamed and banged the drawer shut.

I heard a knock on the door. I quickly wrapped a rough grey-white towel around me. It barely covered my essentials. It must have been left behind by the former tenant.

Oisin and Mozart raced up the concrete steps. She was rosy-cheeked and her gaiety filled up my empty space. I put on the broadest grin. I was a wonderful actress but Mozart looked at me and whimpered. He felt my pain; he was always there for me on this journey.

"Mom, you have black feet!"

I looked down and sure enough, two black feet loomed before me, stained by the dye from my trousers.

"Hey, I look like a penguin!"

We burst out laughing. I waddled around the apartment and Oisin and Mozart followed. We got a bit hysterical, laughing and crying at the same time. But it was a relief to lighten the atmosphere. I wrapped the towel around my daughter's shoulder.

"Mom, I am seeing a little too much of you now," she exclaimed.

I realised that I was standing totally naked in front of my eleven-year-old. She blushed and I ran into the bedroom to put on some underwear.

"I'm decent now."

I did a mad dance in the middle of our new home. I hoped that neighbours from the opposite apartment block could not see into the window. If they did I'd give them a run for their money. I would dance my flamenco and frighten the life out of anyone who dared look in. I stamped and thundered through the whole apartment.

"Mom, now do your belly dance, the special one, please"

I moved my hips and thrust my belly in and out. I rolled my belly like the waves of the sea. Oisin did the shussing sounds. I was breathless.

"Do it again. Do it again," she exclaimed.

I did, and Mozart yapped at my feet. My mood lifted for a while.

Night beckoned and the streetlights shimmered through our bay window. Passers-by rushed home from their work and shoppers were struggling with their awkward parcels. We watched them through our little apartment's eyes. We did not feel part of their world. We lit candles that Oisin found in one of the drawers. We pretended to be in our tent and whispered our hopes and our dreams.

"Mom, it smells funny here," Oisin whimpered. I knew she was missing her fresh large, clean bedroom in suburbia. I enfolded her in a warm hug.

"I'll buy nice freshener in the morning and open all the windows."

"Will we be okay, Mom?"

I took her plump face in my hands and looked into her bright blue eyes.

"Of course we will be. Trust me." I sounded convincing enough.

"Mom, I love you and that is all that matters."

"I love you too."

She snuggled into me. It wouldn't do any harm to let her sleep a few nights with me until she settled in.

In the darkness, I reached out for Mozart's wet nose. He was allowed to sleep at the end of the bed. His little body moved to accommodate two sets of feet under the covers.

Like a buoy at sea, I bobbed about aimlessly. But when I heard Oisin's soft breathing beside me, I knew it had to be different this time. I knew I had to get my act together. I would not mess up this wonderful human being lying beside me. Her strength and purity were like a beacon in my black sea. She would not flounder because of my mistakes. I knew I had not done a bad job with motherhood. But damn it, it was not enough. She deserved the best possible mother to guide her. I vowed to myself to buck up and face all the battles ahead. She had followed me blindly, without hesitation. Her resolve strengthened me. Her golden hair was spread out on her pillow. I blew away some loose strands from her face. She sighed in her sleep and I prayed to God that he would protect her from all the crap that I had been through. I cursed Him. I shook my fist in the darkness. My tears were answered by more darkness descending upon our room. No more light shone through our window. I chose sleep.

My life seemed to have lost direction. I never could find the way, anywhere, not even out of a paper bag, as they say. I could never find my way back. Even going into town was an issue. I dreaded being lost and alone. One day I hoped I would find my way back 'home', back to the real me.

My stay in the Netherlands had not been easy. I felt disconnected and different from the start. I'd had to learn a new language and integrate into a new culture. I took some solace in the fact that I could be someone else in Holland. My Dutch friends had no clue who I really was. How could they? They were very down-to-earth like Lucas. My day to day routine soothed me, I lived with constant highs and lows, as I did my best to please and appease. Lucas had taken control of our lives because I let him. It was easier. I was a willing captive but our marriage paid the price. I had felt I had no choice but to stay. There had never been any choice. Along the way I lost all sense of myself. While I waited for something to happen, months became years and the years were infinite. Increasingly impotent I began to struggle with the smallest things. Even packing for holidays was a nightmare.

Our lifestyle had been comfortable. I had had everything I could want, but I wanted nothing. Surrounded by emptiness every day I lost the ability to desire. I didn't deserve anything anyway. When Oisin had been born, it had been the one light that entered my bleak life. I surrendered even more and let my life be run like a military operation. It was better that way. Towards the end of our marriage, I could not even write a shopping list without assistance.

"Small bananas, not big bananas," Lucas had yelled at me, tearing at his hair in frustration.

"Sorry, love," I'd say and underline the word *small* on my list to be on the safe side. I became what was expected of me again.

Lucas had an undying faith in God but I hated Sundays with a vengeance. Just sitting in a church gave me the creeps. Being part of a congregation forced me to face my childhood memories. I wanted to run, to shout, but I sat there and smiled. After all, Lucas loved me. He would save me from myself. And he did, for nearly twenty years. But the cracks had started to appear when I had lost our baby boy. Or perhaps even earlier? We were opposites and tried to complement each other. However, cultural differences and misunderstandings reared their ugly heads.

As Lucas had gotten thinner, I had gotten fatter, while we both struggled to stay in control. The strain on both of us was evident. I know Lucas's health suffered. He tried to fix and be practical. I tried to create and was not practical at all. How could I be? I had been brought up in a bubble that was my protection. I started to rebel, and the more I rebelled the more his spider's web of control sucked me in. Lucas couldn't help it. When I gave up my job to be a stay-at-home mum, the balance of our relationship shifted. I was not financially independent any more. Our one great common denominator was our beautiful daughter. We had invested all our energies into her.

Over the next few weeks in our new apartment I learned to pay the bills and set up a warm and loving home for us. I went into overdrive. Everybody was proud of me. They thought I was doing wonderfully. But 'proud' did not mean anything to me. It was a word. The feeling associated with that word did not exist. I had spent too many years being disconnected. The meaning of words made them more painful because I longed to feel their emotions.

I went to a writing workshop, thinking I could write a book. I'd call it *Fifty, Fat, Free and Flat Broke*. I laughed hysterically. The words were funny but empty. Even my writing was a compromise. I'd learned to make a joke of how I really felt to make the pain go away. People seemed to find me hilarious and I took comfort in that. I was deeply sad and vulnerable – not funny at all. One day I *would* write that book. Back then, the only thing I thought was that I was ready for the scrap heap.

I needed money desperately and sat down and wrote at least sixty applications for different jobs. I needed to make ends meet until the court case. The court would decide the alimony, but more importantly, the custody of Oisin. Lucas had filed for full custody. I was devastated but had to concentrate on the practicalities. I didn't plan to leave one situation only to be dependent on another. Turlough had been more than generous. It was up to me now.

Rejection after rejection came through the computer or through the letter box. I had to do something. I looked at Mozart. Oisin was at school.

"Well, little comrade, time to go the city and kick some ass with my singing and guitar playing."

Mozart yelped enthusiastically.

I placed Daddy's old grey trilby on the pavement in front of me and closed my eyes. Mozart's warm body was pressed against my legs. It gave me courage and I fought back the feeling of humiliation rising steadily up through my body. I sang a song that I had written many years ago.

"The tears fell from my bewildered brow.

I touched my face and didn't know how,

because the salt of the wind called me to another time, another place."

I felt multiple eyes on me and opened my own to see a crowd gathering. I felt encouraged and sang further. An old lady approached me. Her stockings were practically falling off her stick-like legs. She placed a crisp fifty euro in my hand and her wrinkled hands shook noticeably.

"You sing with your heart and soul," she whispered.

"I couldn't possibly take so much money. My reward is your appreciation," I replied. I sang a song especially for her and waved her off into the gathering crowds. In an hour, I had one hundred euros, which was enough for our groceries and more.

I saw a policeman approaching in the distance.

"A busker has to have a licence to play on the street," he told me.

I packed up hastily and started walking home. I couldn't afford the luxury of getting such a licence.

It started to rain and the gray pools seemed to gush down from the darkened heavens. Mozart whimpered and I tucked him into my wet coat.

"Time to go home, Mozart. Time to do some shopping."

"Ahmed, what's your special today? Have you something cheap and chunky?" I laughed at my local Turkish shopkeeper.

"For beautiful lady, I have good, fresh chicken, very fresh," Ahmed smiled broadly.

I hoped that it was not too fresh. Perhaps he had killed it with his bare hands at the back of the shop! Fatima, his moonfaced wife came to join us. Her coloured head scarf brightened up the dingy shop.

"Sun will shine soon," she slissed through her toothless grin.

I agreed. The sun will come out and I will live to fight another day.

I made a list of the little jobs I had picked up along the way. It was quite a long one. I ran from one job to another and it kept me busy.

a. Go to Sharon's boutique at ten. Open shop for her. Six hours at six euros. Two days.
b. Go to Joanna's second-hand shop Saturday. Three hours at eight euros.
c. Go to V & D department store, Sunday, twenty euros for the afternoon, being toilet lady.
d. Go to Giovanni's pizza place Tuesday and Thursday night from twelve until six in the morning, four euros an hour.
e. Time over: Busk in Kijkduin or at the Passage in The Hague. Irregular work hours.

Fortunately, I had little time left to think but when I did find a few moments of quiet I found myself asking questions, searching, struggling to discover the truth, running movies of my life up to that point in my head as I looked for clues. Meanwhile I kept playing the fool, wearing big colourful hats and coats and layers of gaudy jewellery. I kept my white blonde hair long and let it flow and be my crowning glory. On the outside I was a Golden Princess. My whole life had been played on the stage, where I could greedily gather snippets of attention to feed my emptiness. Emotionally I was at a standstill. I was the court jester who played to everybody's tune. I attracted all the people that I wanted to avoid. I allowed myself to be the victim, the martyr, the life and soul of every party. The pain inside me was so great that at times I wanted to end it all. But I couldn't leave Oisin. She was the only purity in my twisted life. I cut myself to feel alive. Deep slashes in my groin, where no one would see. I thought the knife would make the pain go away but instead it increased the pain I felt inside. Even the knife betrayed me. Its cold metal showed no mercy when I slashed out in despair.

My eating habits had been out of control for many years and I stuffed food into my face to fill the void in my soul. When my mother had died I had no one to tell me what to eat anymore. My life in the Netherlands was very stressful. It is not easy to learn a new language and try to integrate into another culture. I struggled constantly to be heard and understood. My journey to this point had been filled with heartache. Living was painful. I had loved to sing as a child, but as an adult I no longer had the courage to do it alone, so I sang with bands and other people. I always had to have someone telling me what to do.

During those first few weeks in our shabby apartment I had recurring nightmares about my childhood. Frightening scenes flashed before my eyes, with faces I couldn't place. There was violence and pain and inexplicable horror. I couldn't understand where they were coming from.

"Go back to the beginning, Niamh," a voice kept saying, so I sat at the plain dining table with my second-hand laptop and began to write.

CHAPTER 2

TWO
WALKING INTO THE WORLD

I was only two and I tottered through the kitchen on my chubby little legs. My whole world seemed to be this long space of black and white squares. I liked the top of the kitchen table and my fingers just reached the wooden edge. I loved the bright black buttons on the stove. I tried again and again to turn them but a big hand would always reach out and stop me. Everybody seemed to be very tall and I would have to stretch my neck so far back that it almost hurt. I would inevitably fall down with the exertion and have to start all over again. I was in a big world and reached out hungrily to be part of it.

I wore white leather shoes with ankle straps and two white pearly buttons on the sides. My mother and I went to a very chic shop in Dublin called Brown Thomas. The young assistant helped my mother put them on my little feet. I remember seeing their two heads bowed in concentration as they tried to fasten the fine straps. My mother lifted me onto the carpeted floor and I loved the feeling of the soft leather on my feet.

"We will have to get you nice socks to go with them," Mammy said, smiling softly at me. I stood up and took off at a fair pace, running up and down the shop floor between the aisles of shoes.

"There's no stopping her now," the shop assistant laughed. "She'll be flying around the place. You won't be able to catch her."

And she was right. I was determined to run all the way home. My mother had to run after me and grab me before I reached the shop's beautiful brass door, with its giant gold handle in the form of a lion's head.

The lion's golden mane loomed up at me. I could have sworn that I heard it roar at me to "Stop!" I had to hand back my beautiful shoes and watched the shop assistant wrap up our purchase. I had great difficulty seeing my shoes disappear into the candy pink box. White tissue paper enveloped them as the top of the shoebox was firmly closed. My lower lip began to tremble.

"You can put them on when we get home," Mammy said as I clutched her hand. Home, then, seemed such a long way away.

I adored these shoes and ran from one end of our bright kitchen to the other. I loved the hard sounds I made when I was running and the silences when I stopped. I would stand and tap each foot separately before taking off again.

My older brothers, Turlough and Eoghan, would sometimes join in and we'd play Cowboys and Indians. I was always the calf that had to be branded or lassoed. I would run as fast as my little legs could carry me and they would scream, "Howdee, cowboy!" and give chase. Sometimes my mother had to intercede because the cowboys would forget that I was not an animal. The rough and tumble would sometimes be a little too much for me.

"Ah, no boys, go easy there, she's only a baby," she would exclaim.

But I didn't care. My white leather shoes would smile up at me and when the sunlight shone through our large kitchen window, I could almost see my face in the pearly buttons. It was quite a task for my mother to get them off me before putting me to bed. I fell asleep with them on sometimes. My mother took them off while I slept. I dreamt of long roads and hills and stopping to pick daisies to make a daisy chain. Everything was white and shiny.

My mother had a younger brother. Uncle Andrew was ten years her junior. She always looked out for him while they were growing up, largely, I now believe because, my grandparents spent so much time in the local pub. Andrew was in his twenties and was a trendy Mod with a slick black quiff in his hair and he often came to the house with his friends. He didn't take life very seriously and roamed from one job to another. His previous job had been on a Mister Whippy ice-cream van. He would park it outside our house and all the kids in the neighbourhood would hear the clang of the van's song and come for ice-cream.

Uncle Andrew didn't have the heart to take money for the ice-creams. He lasted a week at that job, but it was the best week of our lives. When my brothers and I heard the siren approaching, we'd all line up for our free ice-cream, as if Uncle Andrew were the Pied Piper. My mother was furious.

"Andrew, you're bringing down the tone of the neighbourhood," she said, glaring at him. Uncle Andrew and the Mister Whippy van screeched off down the road with all the children shouting "Whoopee" after it. I tried to keep up but ended up waving at the coloured giant ice-cream cone on the van's rooftop as it disappeared into the distance. My brothers and I would sing along to the Mister Whippy tune and make pretend ice-cream cones out of bits of cardboard and shiny sweet wrappings. It drove our mother mad.

"Larah Dida, Larah Dida," we screeched in unison.

"Jesus, Mary and Joseph, would you sing something else?"

At that stage I thought that those were our real names. I wanted to be called Mary and I wrapped a white sheet around me that I had taken off the clothes' line. It smelled of lavender. I thought the other sheets might be lonely on the line, so I tried to put mine back but I couldn't reach up that high and tottered and teetered as I stretched as high as I could with the crumpled bundle.

"Give me that," my mother said when I couldn't reach, and she pegged it into place. "You are a strange little girl, Niamh, so you are."

She took me back inside into the warm kitchen. I climbed up to look out of the window and saw my sheet moving in unison with the other sheets. I waved at it happily.

Uncle Andrew came to our house with Derek, his tall friend, on many occasions. I missed my father and something in Derek reminded me of him. My father was a seaman and was away for long stretches at a time. Daddy was my anchor in all the madness around me but he would disappear and reappear all the time. It was very confusing for such a young family.

"Your father will be home soon," my mother would say. But "soon" was a word that meant nothing to my brothers and I. "Soon" meant a long, long time.

I would run to Derek and wrap my arms around his long legs. His curly hair shone in the sunlight and I tried to reach up and grab one of his dark curls on his forehead. The more he visited the more intense my love for him grew. I didn't have eyes for anybody else. He would grab me and throw me in the air and I felt such a love for him in my little beating heart.

"Niamh, come over to me," he would say and I would run at such a speed that everybody would laugh. I would bury my head in his leather jacket, which smelled of outside and rainy days. He had a motorbike.

"Stop that!" my mother snapped one day, slapping my fingers away from his long legs. I felt her discomfort but didn't understand it. She made me go and play with my brothers. I didn't want to. I just wanted to embrace this tall, wonderful young man.

"Don't encourage her now," my mother said. Derek stopped opening his arms to me and started ignoring me. His dark brown eyes would avoid making contact with mine. His long lashes flickered in the light. I wanted to make them look at me. I wanted to pull him towards me. But my hands still stung from Mammy's wrath so I didn't. Instead I whimpered. Derek didn't take any notice. I lay on the floor and watched a spider weave his intricate pattern on the ceiling. I wanted him to get closer to Derek too, but in the end, Derek simply disappeared from my life and so did the spider. I watched his black hairy legs run away, leaving me abandoned on the floor. I pointed up at him. Nobody saw him and nobody saw me. My tears were salty and I was thirsty.

The pearly white buttons on my leather shoes ceased to shine but I had no idea why. Whenever Derek did come round, I played in a corner of the kitchen or sat in one of the low cupboards under the sink. I peeped out now and again but I preferred being invisible.

I think that is when I stopped looking out at the world. Seeing what I wanted but not being able to have it taught me not to look. It was better to stay in the dark, alone with my sadness. The darkness of the cupboard was comforting.

"It is for the best," and "she has to learn that…" were whispered just within my earshot. My brothers were told to leave me alone and ignore me. The pearly buttons had lost their sheen, and they felt cold now, there in the musky cupboard. Mammy's dusters and cleaning bottles smelled funny. I wanted to step back out into the light but at the same time I didn't. There in the dark I sang my little songs to entertain myself. There, mixed in with the bleach and the scrubbing brushes, the world was nice to me. I spent more and more time in the sink cupboard.

"Get out into the sunshine," my mother said, dragging me out of the cupboard and forcing me to play outside with my brothers. I longed for my special place and cried.

My mother put locks on the cupboard doors. I scratched at the bright white door to let me in, but it didn't react.

After that I refused to put on my pearly shoes again. My mother forced them onto my wriggling feet, but I howled and screamed until she gave up in frustration. I insisted on walking barefoot everywhere, right up until I went to school. I chose a big pink washing-up bowl to sit in and would move through the kitchen on this.

"You were just too fat to walk," she said.

But I know the truth. It was too painful to walk when I was never able to go where I chose, to Daddy, to Derek, to the washing line, the cupboard. Now my buttons had lost their lustre. It was safer not to move. My washing-up bowl would protect me.

CHAPTER 3

FIVE
SCHOOL STARTS

Daddy came home at last, and brought with him an unusual red pleated skirt and embroidered blouse for me.

"Where did you get that?" I asked, marvelling at the bright colours and the soft fabric.

"Hungary," he replied in his deep baritone voice. I thought he said "hungry" and he growled like a grizzly bear and lunged at me as if to eat me.

The pleats moved when I walked. I counted them constantly to make sure they stayed together. I was afraid they would run away from each other. Daddy said I looked like a walking accordion. I knew it had something to do with music and I sang to my red foreign friend. I danced over the kitchen floor and my father played a gypsy song on his guitar, while I pretended that I was at some faraway place.

My mother was crocheting white knee socks to go with my new outfit. She had spent weeks making them in an intricate flower pattern. I watched the flowers grow and grow, enough to carpet the green patch of grass outside our house like daisies in summer. Their pattern fascinated me and I would put my finger through the fine holes.

"Sure, there will be nothing left of them for your special day," my mother would say, and I would run away and hide behind Daddy's armchair.

"Paddy, she has grown in the time you have been away. Don't forget that now. It's better that she wears a white petticoat underneath to make it look longer," Mammy whispered to Daddy.

"Ah, leave the child alone, Padraicin, aren't her legs long and straight and she's covered, isn't she?" Daddy winked at me.

"But Mammy, my pleats won't dance with me then," I protested.

I knew that when Daddy was at home, he was the boss over Mammy.

"Ah sure, leave her be," said Daddy. "She's covered, isn't she? He repeated it sternly and that was that.

He lit his pipe and the smell of tobacco filled the kitchen. The strong smell made me dance even more. I leant against the powerful arms of my father and drank in his strength and playfulness.

"Padraicin, I am going to make one of my special foreign dishes tonight. We should ask Maeve and Joe over," he said.

There was silence. I saw my mother making a face before going on with her work.

"You can help me cut the vegetables, Niamh," he said, winking at me.

"No, it's too dangerous and I'll have to redo the whole mess," Mammy folded her arms and looked at him seriously.

"Let her learn. It won't do her any harm."

"Agh, Paddy, you always make life complicated when you come home."

Daddy raised his hands to the ceiling and rolled his eyes at me, then smiled, picked up his guitar and started playing a sea shanty. I skipped barefoot over the kitchen floor and my mother let out one of her big breathy sighs. Dad laid his guitar on the kitchen table, grabbed her by the waist and brought her to him. She smiled as he whisked her over the floor.

"More, more!" I shouted as they waltzed down the kitchen.

That night Daddy got out his beloved mandolin and played for us in the kitchen. It was Saturday and that was bath night. Daddy lifted us up one by one onto the kitchen table. We knew that it was time for Daddy to go away again. His mandolin came out on these occasions. He played haunting melodies and we listened, captured by the sounds. I felt all squeaky clean but I had a heavy heart.

"Daddy, will you teach me how to play, then you won't have to go away for another while?" I pleaded with him, standing between his legs, strumming the strings until the humming reached my chest.

Turlough and Eoghan also pleaded with him to stay. They piped up: "Daddy, you will miss Turlough's First Holy Communion."

"Now, do you know what I have made for us all? Cream crackers with fresh strawberry jam." Mammy softened the situation. Daddy left the kitchen.

My father had to go to sea the day before my first day at school. I said goodbye in my heart as the taxi sped away. We were never allowed to come to the door to wave him off. It was too difficult for all concerned. The front door closed and I heard my mother softly crying in the upstairs bedroom. I listened to her gasps and sat on the stairs waiting for the sounds to stop. My brothers continued playing noisily in the hallway, pushing and shoving each other as they skated in their socks between the front door and the kitchen. I hummed softly to myself and discovered that it helped me forget the muffled whimpers I could hear coming from behind Mammy's bedroom door. It stopped. I ran down the stairs and waited. Mammy emerged, bleary-eyed but cheerful.

"Now, what are we going to have for dinner tonight?" she asked, beaming at us.

"Egg and Mammy's home-made chips," we replied.

Mammy frowned slightly at me and then we ran into the kitchen to watch her peel the potatoes. I hoped that I would be allowed a big portion tonight. After all, Daddy had just left us yet again and we needed cheering up.

We were shooed out of the kitchen and told to play nicely until our dinner was ready. I was relieved. It was too hard to see my mother's pained face trying to be cheerful. She didn't look like Mammy. Her eyes were red and her smile was empty and dead. My dolly, Ruby, had the same look and she scared me sometimes. I didn't want to be scared of my mammy.

I glanced out the living room window and saw our neighbour trimming his side of the hedge. His young son was helping him. They both wore spectacles and the light caught their glasses and reflected against my window. Their heads bobbed up and down whilst the sharp blades did their work. Pieces of green exploded in every direction. I hoped that the end result would look crooked. Their precision annoyed me. I hoped that Daddy would let me help him trim our side of the hedge when he came home. Our hedge started to appear untidier and untidier as they worked. I knew that Mammy would have to work on ours now. I was annoyed at the idea and stuck my tongue out at the neighbour's son. He made a grotesque face back at me and I was startled. I nearly fell off our large grubby overstuffed settee. Luckily, it was bouncy and I regained my balance and jumped up and down holding on to the window ledge. I made one last effort to frighten him. His father looked up and wagged his finger at me. I ducked down under the ledge and gasped. My brothers were playing Cowboys and Indians and ran past me.

"Will you both shut up?" I screamed at them, putting my hands over my ears.
Mammy appeared from upstairs and headed towards the kitchen. I followed and remained silent.

"Please don't let her see the hedge today," I muttered to myself. Things were tense enough with Daddy gone and school the next day.

"Dinner is ready!" came her voice, and I was saved.

We sat in silence and ate. Mammy never ate with us but watched over us, standing against the sink with her arms folded.

"Niamh, don't eat too much or you will be sick," she said. "And that's all I need right now."

I was afraid to eat any more and pushed my plate away. I watched my brothers hungrily dip their bread in the bright yellow yokes. I would have loved to do that too. The ache in my stomach started to grow.

"Mammy, I have a pain in my tummy," I said.

"See, I told you so," she replied. "You ate like a gannet and now you're paying the price."

"But Mammy, I'm hungry."

"You're not. You only think you are. You won't fit into your new outfit for school."

But then she regretted saying it and gave me a big hug.

"Do you want some ice-cream?" she asked. I did not know whether to say "yes" or "no". Mammy looked confused and so did I. I decided to refuse.

I spent the rest of the evening with my pink rubber water bottle pressed against my tummy. Its warmth helped me feel a little better. I was so hungry but dared not ask for food. My tummy rumbled and it felt ticklish. I thought of the runny yellow yoke and dipping my buttered bread into its sticky centre. I fell asleep hoping that I would be allowed to have porridge the next morning. Mammy had said I could if my tummy grew smaller. I felt my tummy with my palm but my belly button got in the way. This small hole frightened me so I patted my tummy goodnight.

My mother held her breath, as Turlough helped her with the long silver zip at the back of her dress. I willed the zip to follow his long slender fingers. This was Mammy's 'thin' dress. What that meant was that she had eaten awful dark brown crackers for weeks on end, so that the dress would fit her on my special day.

"I will fit into this black dress if it kills me," she had been saying for weeks.

Eoghan, who was older than me by a year but smaller, held on to Mammy's waist. He felt he was helping by pushing my mother into the dress. I bit my lip anxiously and my mother smiled triumphantly. It was a tight black dress and she looked beautiful.

Her blond shoulder-length hair caught rays of light through our kitchen window. She asked me to hand over her 'cherry' hat. We called it that because it was the colour of cherries. It was small and dainty and fitted at the side of her head. She gave us one of her rare smiles. You see, Mammy had big black gaps between her teeth. She was terrified to go to the dentist and Daddy had given up telling her to go. She smiled at me broadly and I shivered ever so slightly because I thought the gaps looked like black liquorice bits. When we played pirates, we would stick black liquorice on our teeth. I felt ashamed that I had thought about this and watched Mammy put her hand in front of her mouth. I wanted to tell her not to. I felt a pain in my chest and touched the hem of her dress for reassurance. My brothers and I watched her put her lipstick on. It was cherry red like her hat. We loved when she pouted onto the tissue and we saw the outline of her lips on the soft white tissue paper.

I was also dressed and ready to go. I gazed down at my bright red T-bar shoes and thought they matched very nicely with Mammy's lipstick.

"My two golden princesses," I could hear my father saying.

We set off to drop my brothers off at their school first. It was a small boys' school at the edge of town. It was not run by the priests. My father was against sending them to the priests for primary school. Unfortunately, the nearest school for girls was the local convent. Otherwise Mammy would have to get a bus and take me all the way over to the other side of town. There was a Protestant school nearby but we were Catholic and they would not accept me for enrolment.

"Bloody religion, it will be the downfall of this country," Daddy would say.

The big grey stone convent building suddenly appeared out of nowhere. I thought it looked like a castle.

"Mammy, I see blackbirds over there on the tree!" I exclaimed.

It was a huge, broad oak tree and I touched its bark as we passed. It felt rough and crumbly. The blackbirds flew away as we walked further up the long driveway. It was misty and cold and I heard other sounds behind us. They were the footsteps of other parents and children. I heard whispering and now and again, a whimper. I clung to my elegant mother.

There were strange little stones all the way up the driveway.

"Mammy, what are these little stones called?"

"They are called gravel and it took trucks and more trucks to place them on the ground like that."

"Trucks and more trucks and more trucks," I repeated.

I made up a song and I found the word *gravel* a funny name and tried to rhyme it with other words, which proved difficult. I heard my new crimson shoes scrunching under me to the rhythm of my new song:

"Crunch goes the scrunch under my shoes
Scrunch goes the crunch to my new school."

"Clarks shoes are the best for developing young feet," the lady in the shop had said.

My mother had counted out the pound notes and I had counted with her. The assistant had said I was "a clever little girl" and wrapped my new purchase in white tissue paper. I had been allowed to carry the bag home. I looked down at my shoes and felt safe. My mother liked that the name Clarks was on the bag.

"Make sure you keep the name on the outside," she had said. I knew she hoped that our neighbour, Mrs McNamara, would see us walking up the road from behind her lacy curtains. I had walked proudly, swinging the bag to and fro to the tempo of our steps.

Other mothers and children followed us up the long path. I saw some mothers staring at us and looking away. They whispered and elbowed each other as if there was something funny going on. I looked up at my Mammy and she held her head high and walked very elegantly in her pointed black patent-leather shoes. She dragged me a little along the way. She was clearly in a hurry and I took long steps to keep up with her. I hoped that we were not late.

The dark oak panels inside the old convent were polished and smelled of Mammy's dust cloth at home. The brown parquet floors were slippery and I held on to Mammy's hand tightly. My shoes seemed to want to slide over the floors.

"Behave yourselves, new shoes!" I admonished them, trying hard to put one foot in front of the other to calm them down.

"Will you stop that talking to yourself, Niamh," Mammy said through gritted teeth and a big smile.

There was an air of nervousness and the mothers were trying to be light and frivolous. I squeezed my mother's hand tightly. A wave of blackness came closer at us. Six nuns approached us. Their darkness was only broken only by their white headpieces and pale faces.

"Where's their hair, Mammy?"

"Sshh," she whispered.

The swish of their robes echoed through the corridor and the nuns told us to follow them and turned a corner. I skipped and hopped because it sounded nice and hollow against the wooden floorboards.

"Sshh," my mother said and we entered my new world. The classroom door shut behind us.

Every child was given a place to sit. There was a roll call and my name was called out.

"Niamh Orfhlaith Ni Bhroin."

The nun's face was old and stern. She tried to smile but it looked more like my doll, Ruby's, smile. She repeated my name and looked at me through her round-rimmed spectacles, placed on her nose now. I was frightened but didn't cry. Children whimpered all around me and anxious mothers tried to soothe them. The shushing sounds reminded me of the sea. I would often put my big conch shell to my ear and Daddy would listen with me.

"Ssssssss, listen to the sea," he'd say.

"We will just call her Niamh here," the nun said to my mother. "Niamh Orfhlaith" is just too much of a mouthful."

My mother did not look pleased and the other mothers seemed to whisper and smile to each other. I gave Mammy a smile. She seemed to need one. She put her dainty forefinger to her cherry red lips and I looked away.

The nuns told all the mothers to leave and I bravely sat in my seat whilst other children screamed and howled. I waved a gentle wave to Mammy and blew her a kiss. She caught it in the sunlight and was gone.

Mother Joseph was her name and her piercing brown eyes took us all in.

"Ursula, your mother used to come to school here. I hope you will be as good a pupil as she was." She smiled at Ursula, who was sitting beside me.

The nun's blackness approached me and I smiled up at her.

"Stand up," she said, and pulled down my short little red skirt. I heard something tear as the pleats came away from the waistband. My skirt. My beautiful red skirt given to me by my Daddy when he came back from a place called Hungary.

"You look like a *whore*," said Mother Joseph.

I may not have understood the meaning of the word but I saw the disdain on her face. I *felt* the word and that was enough. From that day forward I knew I was different.

"Niamh Orfhlaith, is it?" she continued. "Well, we won't stand for people who get above their station here. That's not even a saint's name. It's the name of a whore."

My father had chosen my name. It came from the legend of Tir na Nog (the land of eternal youth). Niamh Chinn Oir ('Niamh of the golden hair') was a princess in the story. I was his golden princess. I said nothing.

I felt the nun's old hands pulling at my skirt again. Each time I heard more material rip.

"My daddy bought it for me," I cried. "It came from a faraway place."

The snuffling children became silent. They all focused on my beautiful skirt. I fingered my St Christopher's medal that Mammy had pinned onto my vest that morning. She had said it would protect me. The cold steel did not warm up in my hands.

"Sit down, whore!" Mother Joseph growled and swept away. The rough black cloth brushed against my cheekbone. It smelled dusty and old.

"But ... my skirt moves when I dance," I squeaked.

I sat at my desk and looked down the inkwell. It looked like the thick black feeling I had in my heart and my tummy. I hummed a tune. Mother Joseph suddenly reappeared from nowhere and towered over me.

"What did you say?" she spat.

But I couldn't manage a word. The long bamboo cane smashed down on my folded hands, catching my knuckles.

"We do not tolerate idle dreamers in this school," she shouted.

I was dragged into the corner and a big coned hat was placed on my head.

"Repeat after me..." she said to the other children. "Niamh is stupid and a whore."

I closed my eyes and counted the beautiful butterflies flying around my head. Their brilliant colours made me dizzy. I threw up all over the floor.

"Clean up this foul mess and ask a friend to help you," Mother Joseph sneered, her yellow teeth gleaming like those of the wolf in *Little Red Riding Hood*. My daddy had brought the book home for me and we had spent hours reading it together.

"Daddy, come home and take me away from here," I whispered into the air around me, hoping it would carry my message to him.

The children shied away from me and my wretched stink. I chose the girl nearest to me. Ursula had brown freckles and a nice smile. She cried as we walked down the long corridor to find some cloths. A huge grandfather clock chimed the quarter hour and we both jumped with fright and scurried faster. I looked down at my crimson T-bars and saw splashes of white. Mammy had said that I was allowed to eat all my porridge that morning. Hard lumps stuck onto my white crocheted socks, filling up some of the holes between the daisies. I stooped and tried to pick them away.

"You made me cry," Ursula said. I put my arm around her and told her about the seashell from my father.

I didn't deserve to be consoled. I chose not to be. My red pleated skirt flapped around my knees. The seams had given away and my pleats did not follow me any more. I put my finger through one of the holes, widening it. I was glad Daddy wasn't there to see me.

My mother took one look at my dishevelled appearance.

"What happened to you?" she asked.

She had collected me on her old black bicycle. I did not answer and she did not ask any more questions. I climbed up on the bicycle behind her. My white underpants were peeping through and I felt ashamed suddenly and huddled closer as the movement of the bike soothed me. I held my skirt together until we got home. I felt a song coming up from the bottom of my stomach:

"Bike, bike, cycle with all your might
Away from the blackness of the night."

I knew then that Mammy could not help me. She cried when we got home. I put my arm around her. I was alone.

"I told your father that you should have worn a petticoat," she said. "We don't want any trouble with those nuns. Wait until your father gets home. Wait until you father gets home."

These words echoed in the kitchen and my mother put her hands to her head. I reached out to console her.

"Go on off and play now," she said.

I left her and turned around to see her rocking to and fro. Her dainty fingers clung onto the kitchen sink. Her honey-blond hair hid her face so I could not see her expression, but I could imagine it all right.

"Mammy, I'm sorry. Mammy, I'm sorry," I stammered.

I willed her to reappear from under her hair, but got no reply. The dripping tap that Daddy had not had time to fix seemed to want to say something to me. I felt a song coming up in me:

"Drip, drip goes the tap
It's running down Mammy's back."

I had to go back to school the next day, and the next and the next.

I learned to disassociate myself from the daily cruelty by living in a parallel world. My own world was kinder to me. My life at home and at school was reality. Daddy came and fixed that world when he could, but his long absences became an open wound. I gave up longing for him. It was better not to expect anything and to be happy with the crumbs that were thrown to me.

CHAPTER 4

SIX
PARTING THE RED SEA

"Make way for the individual," Sister McAletta roared.

I did not know what she meant but meaning did not matter. I knew that from experience. It was the *way* she said it. The children parted in front of me like the Red Sea I'd heard about in the Bible. I walked alone.

I thought about how Daddy had once explained to me that the Red Sea is actually very blue.

I felt cold and frightened but I walked down the corridor with dignity. I imagined Jesus standing beside me and we walked together through the sandy seabed. I picked up imaginary shells and smelled the salty air. I heard the seagulls.

"Daddy, is it going to rain now?"

"Yes, they are calling for the rain and it will come soon," his voice boomed. Glimpses of my strength shone through. The nun grabbed me by the hair and pushed me in front of her.

"Let the *individual* walk the walk of the whore of Babylon," she yelled.

I walked in a straight line, my head held high. Sister McAletta smacked my face with the flat of her hand so hard that I fell.

"Daddy, shall I pick some seashells for you as well?"

The gulls circled around me, their shrieks high pitched. Then they disappeared.

The children's eyes avoided me. They were just happy not to be in my position. I got up slowly and walked the rest of the long corridor. The face of Jesus with his glowing heart followed me. I hated that painting, his white robes and bare feet.

"The Sacred Heart died for us all," Mother Joseph's voice rang in my ears. We will all have to pay for our sins."

Jesus seemed to sneer at me and I thought the corridor would never end. I was pushed forward by unseen hands and welcomed any help I could get. It made the journey shorter. I fell again and I felt the children walking over my back, one by one. I instinctively lay down as flat as possible to lessen the pain. Some hesitant shoes tried to avoid my back and hopped over my outstretched arms quickly but they were made to retrace their steps and walk over my back again. Whimpering children were pushed forward again and again.

"Let her feel her disgrace. Whores have to be punished," snapped Mother Joseph.

Silence ensued and I tried to get up, but I hadn't the strength. I held my tears in a safe place.

Mother Joseph pulled me up by my hair and spat in my face. Her spit rolled down my swollen cheek and stopped in the fold of my neck. I wiped it away with my sleeve and I wished that I were dead. I begged anybody to take me away but again no one answered. I sang in my head:

"I wish I were dead with a hole in my head
I wish I were free to drown in the Red Sea
I wish somebody would listen to me."

My mother collected me at the school gates. She lifted me onto the back of her bicycle.

"What happened to your cheek?" she asked.

"I fell Mammy. On the seashore. The Red Sea took me and I nearly drowned."

She looked at me strangely. She was used to my healthy imagination.

"Don't be telling lies now," she said. "Just keep your head down and don't be cheeky at school. I love you Niamh but wait until Daddy gets home. Let's see what he has to say about it. He'll sort it out. He will," she sighed. She promised that I could have a piece of the apple pie she had just baked. We sang all the way home. I thought I felt better but I was not sure.

I felt every bump on the road that day. I held onto my mother's waist and watched as her elegant pumps moved round and round. My long legs dangled. I didn't have the energy to place them in the steel stirrups. I closed my eyes and felt the rhythm of the bicycle. It helped ease my aching face and back. I looked up to the blue sky and the white fluffy clouds followed us. I counted them all the way home:

"Fluffy, fluffy clouds follow me home
I'll put you in my ice-cream cone."

The smell of my mother's baking wafted through the house. It was a homely smell and I drank it in. My elder brothers came in from school and sat at the kitchen table. They were each given a large slice of apple pie. They started to tell us about their day at school.

"Niamh, it's better that you don't have any tart. It might make you sick," my mother said. "You will be better off in the long run because little girls should not get fat."

I was given a dry crust of bread and sat opposite my brothers.

Moist apple dripped down Eoghan's face. I wanted to reach out and lick it. Turlough helped himself to a second piece of pie.

"Eat up now," Mammy said to him. "You are too thin. We can't have the neighbours saying that you are not well fed."

He took my mother's advice and demolished the fat slice. I avoided his gaze. He was oblivious to my longing. I wished that I were him. I wanted to be a boy. I wanted to feel the apple melting in my mouth, to lick my lips and say:

"Mammy, it's lovely apple tart. May I have another slice?"

Suddenly Mammy offered me a slice. She felt guilty for having given me dried crusts. I did not know whether this was a trick or not. If I accept, will she acknowledge that I am fat? I thought. If I refuse, will she be happy that I have such good self-control?

I left the answer up to her. She placed a huge slice of apple tart in front of me. I decided to eat half. That way, everybody would be happy.

I saw Mammy scrutinising me and she seemed happy with the compromise.

"Good girl, only eat until you feel full."

The truth was that I did not know the meaning of the word 'full'. I was always hungry.

I was sick at school and hungry at home. That's all I knew.

I was Niamh. I didn't even consider myself a girl. I was the thing that was beaten up and ridiculed at school. The other girls didn't seem to have that problem. I was the thing that didn't deserve a piece of apple pie. I was the *thing* that nobody listened to. I sang another little song in my head:

"Apple pie is not good for me
It will make me fat and unhappy."

I went upstairs to my room and placed my seashells in my drawer. I knew they weren't real, but that wasn't important.

"Daddy will want to see them later," I said to myself.

My father was away for a long, long time. Eventually my conch shell did not interest me anymore. I put it in the back of my wardrobe and closed the door.

I lay on my bed and read *Little Red Riding Hood*. The wolf grinned at me. I punched him in the face and threw the book away from me. It landed on the floor. I saw Red Riding Hood smiling up at me from a distance. Her pretty basket was full of nice things for her grandmother. I imagined all the food that I would eat in her world. I tasted the fruity jam and fresh bread that stuck out of her basket. The jam stuck to my face and I traced its stickiness down to my chin. I felt sick. I just wanted to sleep and dream of Daddy coming home.

"Niamh, come downstairs. Dinner will be ready soon," my mother called.

The smell of delicious shepherd's pie wafted into my nostrils but I didn't want to smell it. Would I be allowed to have some of it tonight? Would I be allowed to eat the same as my brothers? I started plucking the loose woollen threads on my bedspread. I imagined the threads to be Mother Joseph's eyelashes and plucked so furiously that a hole started to appear. I looked into the gap and saw my pink flannel sheet. My eyelashes brushed against the soft cotton. I liked the feathery feel and spent some time peering through the hole. I then rearranged the bedclothes to cover the hole. This was my special secret hole.

When I thought of returning to school the next day, my back started to hurt. In my mind I counted the footprints that had landed on my back. Eithne's shoes had been soft but Eileen's had been very hard with small leather heels. They were new shoes with neat little bows. Katherine's shoes were patent leather with shoelaces. Poor Ursula had to jump on my back a lot but she was a light little thing. I heard her crying and she whispered "sorry" when Mother Joseph was not looking. I hoped that my back would not be too bruised. If Mammy saw, I would say that we had played a game of doctors and patients; that I had been the patient and the children had pinched me. That story had worked before.

Either my mother saw the bruises and didn't acknowledge them or they did not exist at all. I chose to believe the latter.

I remember playing over at Vivienne's. She made me be the patient and pinched me and stuck me with needles until I cried out in pain. My arms were covered with bruises.

"Everybody can see your arms," Mammy had said angrily. "It looks so ugly, all those blue marks. Why did you let her do that to you?"

I didn't know. All I remember was that I felt no pain. It wasn't until I saw my mother's reaction that I started feeling the tingling of the purple spots on my arms. I realised that I didn't need to worry about getting into trouble over the bruises on my back. Nobody could see them. My mother would not be as angry.

"Oh God, wait until your daddy gets home," she would merely exclaim.

"It doesn't matter Mammy, honestly, it doesn't matter," I said. Daddy would not be home for quite a while though. My young life was spent waiting. My mother's life was on hold. I understood that from an early age. Daddy fixed everything when he came home. That was her coping mechanism and mine was not to rock the boat too much. I continued to find my own ways of coping. I rarely played outside in the sunshine. Instead I'd escape into my brothers' Enid Blyton *Famous Five* books. I drank in their adventures. This made my own life bearable.

One day though, I was outside with all the children and I told a story and they were fascinated by it. I sat on our front wall in the garden, the children surrounding me. It was a lovely feeling being listened to and my stories became very popular indeed.

Mammy wanted me to stick close to her. She pottered around the house and I followed like a puppy dog. She would make up one bed and I would sit on the other and then change places while she made up the other bed.

Her world was my world and my brothers were outside that world. They came and went and played outside. They made noise and ate heartily. Now and again I would interact with them. I envied them. Sometimes I had feelings of great anger when they came screaming through the house. There was a never-ending cycle of noisy boys. I yelled at them to be quiet so I could read my books.

"Little girls should be seen and not heard," Turlough told me in a remarkable imitation of Mammy's voice, hands on hips, silent and still for a moment before cuffing his friend round the ear and baiting him into another game of chase.

Inside my head I begged, shouted and pleaded. I sang whole songs of protest that nobody heard.

CHAPTER 5

SEVEN
LEFT-HANDED

The Catholic Church in the early '60s had its own policy about left-handed children. They all had to be converted into right-handed people. The theory was that Satan sat on the left-hand side of Jesus and no true followers of Christ would want to sit there now would they?

We all had to learn how to knit and that was very difficult for me, left-handed as I was. I simply could not get to grips with the coordination.

Sister McAletta loomed over me and every time I used my left hand instead of my right, the cane or steel ruler would deal out its punishment. My knuckles were so bruised that they took on a permanent purple hue. It got to the stage where I couldn't knit at all. So I sat there, waiting for the punishment to be handed out.

"Here we go; the daughter of Satan has dropped a stitch."

"Who are you? Yes, Satan's whore and confidante, I'm addressing you."

"You will feel God's mercy in the power of my sword."

The cane would come down on my bruised knuckles.

"Do not play with this Jezebel," Sister McAletta

would say to the other children. "She will take you to hell with her."

I used to run after some of the children at playtime, threatening to drag them into my den of sin. Some were genuinely frightened but others found it exciting and funny. We accepted the situation and made the best of it. I was so accustomed to being beaten that a day without a beating was a strange day indeed. It was better to be beaten and get it over than deal with the anticipation of a beating.

It proved so difficult to write with my right hand that I dared not write at all. Dipping my fountain pen into the inkwell was almost impossible. I always sucked up too much ink and blobbed big blue stains everywhere. My blotting paper was full of blue patterns. I spent more time looking at the stains than writing. The squiggly patterns resembled the way I felt, without direction. Their blueness took on different faces and the blots became my friends. When the cane came down on my weary hands, I stared at my new friends until the onslaught was over.

Sister McAletta would stand in front of me and pull my flaxen curls.

"Jezebel, write with your right hand," she'd say.

Sometimes, she would hold my left arm and twist it behind my back. The pain was intense. Still I could not write properly.

"You are struggling to fight against good," she would say, grasping my arm while I gasped from the pain. "The devil is drawing you into his lair."

Eventually, I gave up the struggle, placed my head down on my desk, put my index finger into the inkwell and made pretty patterns on my blotting paper. I longed for the devil to take me and be done with it. I wondered whether Sister McAletta would leave me alone if I made a pact with him; if I became his whore.

"I have sold my soul to the devil," I shouted one day. "He is going to take me to his lair of thieves and whores. I am going to sit on his right-hand side, and bugger you to hell!"

The children, astonished, were told to go back to their work.

I remember the silence in the classroom and that I was put in a corner for the rest of the day. Left alone I felt peaceful and sang in my head all day:

"Bugger the angels and bugger the dead
I'm sitting with Satan and eating brown bread."

I smelled my mother's freshly baked brown bread. I ate it with my red-horned friend and we did a jig together. He found it difficult to dance because of his hooves and so I linked arms with him to help. His smelly breath sickened me but I told him that he could borrow my toothpaste whenever he liked. His eyes shone through me and I was terrified that he would take me to his lair.

"God would forgive you if only you behaved yourself," I told him. He disappeared and I opened my eyes to find the whole class staring back at me. Sister McAletta pushed me further into the corner, this time with my back to the class.

"Do not look at the daughter of Satan," she said. "She has powers of deception."

I stared at the blank wall and then closed my eyes.

The devil and I continued our jig until the school bell rang. I told Mister Red (which was my new nickname for the red-eyed monster) that we would be friends for now and that he was not to try and take me to his den. He agreed. He told me that he would wait until I was a bit older. I said I would think about it.

He disappeared and I turned, legs aching, to face an empty class. Sister McAletta peered around the class door.

"Has the whore not left yet?" she said. "Good, I want to speak to your mother anyway. Get out of my sight, you disgusting excuse for a human being."

I tried to run past her but she caught me by the arm. I stared at her unblinkingly.

"You had better watch out because Mister Red was eating brown bread with me and he will only take me to his lair when I am older. He might take you to his den of whores instead."

She was flabbergasted and let go of my arm as if it were red hot.

"You are mad as well as a whore,' she said. "They will lock you up in the madhouse. Yes, the madhouse, the madhouse, the MADHOUSE…"

She swept off into the distance. I stood there and felt some sort of victory but became confused when I realised I might be taken away to the madhouse. My long legs ran down the corridor and my echoing footsteps seemed to chase me. I had to see the sunlight. I dashed towards the broad oak door that was the convent entrance.

My mother was waiting for me outside on her bicycle. I was so relieved to see her and hurried towards safety.

Unfortunately, Sister McAletta had gotten there first.

"I want to have a little chat about your daughter," she said in her best voice, suggesting my mother follow her back into the convent. "She said some disgraceful things today…"

I had to wait outside and stand by my mother's bike. I watched the two figures disappear into the darkness behind the convent door. My mother turned and looked at me. The look on her face spoke louder than words. It shrieked 'What the hell did you do now?' I shrugged my shoulders and played with the big brass button-like bell on her bike. I kept on ringing it because the sound blanked everything else out. It had a lovely clanging sound and I hummed a tune to myself.

My mother said nothing on the way home and the bicycle ride was very long indeed. In the hallway, she smacked me on the back of the legs.

"For God's sake Niamh, do what she says. I can't cope with trouble. Your father won't be home for another six months. Now we will all have to go to Mass on Sunday. Jesus, that's all we need."

We never usually went to Mass. My mother hated it. She had put on a lot of weight and could not face being seen until she had lost the weight again. This could take a while. But she knew we had to show our faces this time because the local parish priest would have been informed of my conduct. Like me, Mammy had a healthy imagination. Father Hans often visited the convent to hear all the news about our 'little souls'. I could imagine him being treated to holy tea and Sister McAletta telling him all about my sins. I could see their faces scrunch up as they munched on crucifix-shaped biscuits. I fantasised about Reverend

Mother choking on her biscuit as all was revealed to her. I saw her eyes popping out of their sockets and Father Hans and Sister McAletta popping them back into her wizened old head. Blood dripped off her eyeballs into the holy tea. They all dunked their crucifixes into their bloody tea.

I got into such a state about it that my poor mother was convinced my sins would be announced from the pulpit. I seemed to have whisked her along on this trail of overinflated imagination.

"I regret to inform you that in this parish there is a family that worships the devil," she imagined the priest saying.

But then she came back to earth and exclaimed, "Sod them all."

And then we burst out laughing with relief at her verdict and my feeling of doom and gloom evaporated, at least for a while. We went to Mass though, just in case.

"It's a sort of insurance policy," my mother explained, "just in case something was said."

I didn't mind. I wanted to say hello to the Blessed Virgin and her baby.

The incident was not mentioned, so my mother, brothers and I sneaked out of the church when it was time for Communion. Timing was of the essence. My mother gave us a sign and we escaped like thieves in the night. We ran down the road, my mother giggling all the way home. She liked a little drama in her otherwise predictable life. I loved the sound of her infectious laugh and wished that we would hear more of it.

We avoided our neighbours too. They would be standing outside the church after the mass, gossiping. My mother hated standing outside and gossiping. The chances were that the gossip was about us. My mother was a fine figure of a woman and her husband was away at sea. The other women would have loved to have something to talk about.

But my mother was a proud and faithful woman and did her best to ensure that they had as little as possible to say about her. Her children were always immaculately dressed and walked tall and straight. Perhaps we looked haughty and from a different world? We were colourful though. I always wore beautiful clothes that my mother had chosen with great care. My father always brought home unusual items. We were the first children to wear duffle coats. He had brought them home from Canada. Mine was bright red with beautiful ivory toggles. My brothers' were navy blue and very smart indeed.

After that I started writing with my right hand and began to stammer.

My father came home from sea and saw the state I was in. I couldn't manage to speak coherently. My tongue would not let the words escape but instead sat in my mouth like a swollen slug.

"For God's sake, Leonardo da Vinci was left-handed and so was the Blessed Virgin herself," he said.

My mother raised an eyebrow at that.

"I am going down to that lot and I am going to kill them. Did you see the state of that child? Padraicin, what the hell is going on here?"

His voice boomed through the house. Although we knew it was a lot of hot air, my brothers and I ducked for cover, just in case.

I sat on Daddy's lap as he spoon-fed me creamed mashed potatoes. I held onto him as if life depended on it. His muscled thighs supported me like big tree trunks. His presence made me stronger. He sang to me and I ate heartily.

I was never sick when he was home. The added bonus was that I was allowed to eat what I liked and I got stronger and stronger. Daddy made up recipes and he would cook exotic dishes for us. I was his *sous-chef*.

"Daddy, what did Confucius say?" I would ask.

"Confucius says to keep your bowels open and your mouth closed."

We would roar with laughter. I don't remember my mother being in the kitchen. I think she was glad to get a break. My brothers helped when it suited them.

"Any volunteers?" my father would ask, and they would run away as if their life depended on it.

Daddy could be a little bit impatient. His enthusiasm got the better of him. I understood that. His passion for cooking made him that way.

"Where's that knife? Are you not finished cutting those potatoes yet, Niamh?"

I didn't mind. Our time was precious and I wanted to savour every moment we had together.

Strong smells emerged from the kitchen and we would all sit down to sample his culinary expertise. Even Mammy would join us.

"Now Padraicin, sit down there and sample this dish."

he would say. I loved seeing us all together as a family. I stored the moment in my memory so that I could relive it in those miserable times.

Daddy went to have a chat with the nuns. I waved him off down the road.

"Dad will put them straight," Mammy assured me. "He will tell them a thing or two."

I looked at my mother, unconvinced. She had kitchen paper rolled up in a ball in her hands. She always had kitchen paper in her hands. She hated anything sticky. She scrunched it up and smiled at me.

I don't know what was said between my father and the nuns but for the coming months I was left to my own devices. I was allowed to write with my left hand. My speech returned and my stammer disappeared. I could relax for a while, though every day I would turn to him.

"Daddy, you are not going away, are you?" I'd ask.

"No, not for a long time yet," he would reply.

But the inevitability of that day hung over me like a black cloud.

"When is your father going back to sea, Niamh?" Sister McAletta would ask, her eyes meeting mine. She rubbed her hands as if they were very cold but I knew what she meant. She knew that I knew. She continued with the lesson. I imagined stapling her long black garment to the ground. When she moved, it would tear to reveal the body of a serpent, a green one with a long flickering tongue. I could think like that because I felt stronger in myself. Daddy was home.

When he left, my hell began again and was often even worse than before. My reality was all about survival so I relied on fantasy to get me through. Sometimes, I mixed up which was which. My blackened knuckles had become hard and calloused and I accepted whatever was dished out to me. There is nothing worse than getting used to being beaten. It slowly takes away every bit of your dignity and self-esteem. I was too young to realise that this would have major repercussions later on in life.

CHAPTER 6

EIGHT
FIRST CONFESSION

The catechism had been drilled into us. We had to make our first confession the night before Communion. So, on a dark October Saturday night, we marched into the church. I could have made my communion in May but my mother had kept me back a year to recover from my stammering. She felt that it would be better for me. Unfortunately, it made me feel even worse. I had to deal with Sister McAletta for another year. The other children were seven and I was going on eight.

"There are venial sins and mortal ones. Venials are for small things like a little white lie. The mortal sins are for murderers, adulterers, rapists and WHORES," Sister McAletta paused and stared directly at me. The whole class followed her eyes and their stares landed on me.

I looked ahead , praying that the priest would forgive my sins.

The church chandeliers gave off a brilliant light and I followed the other children inside. I was tall for my age and I remember trying to reach up to one of the burning lights. I saw the Blessed Virgin Mary looking down at me with the baby Jesus in her arms. I felt warm and tingly inside because she looked so kind and pure. A novice nun pushed me into the confessional box. Sister

McAletta smirked at me. It terrified me further. The darkness invaded my soul. The steel grid that separated us opened and the priest waited.

"Bless me, Father for I have sinned," I said. "This is my first confession."

"Tell me your sins, my child," he replied.

I couldn't answer. I felt imprisoned and I concentrated on the steel bars in front of me. Their silver colour was the only brightness in the confessional box. He repeated his question a few times but I remained silent.

"Say something, you stupid lump of a girl."

Still I could not speak. "I have heard about you," he shouted. "You are the one that gives them so much trouble. Get out of my sight!"

The young nun whisked me out of the confessional. The children stared. Sister McAletta threatened the other children with penances if they didn't go in an orderly fashion into the confessional. The next child went in and the others sat waiting and whimpering.

"You stupid whore," she said, shoving me into a corner. "Stay there until the others are finished."

I didn't mind. Mary was there and the baby Jesus reached out to me. I did not reach back. I knew better. My bitten fingernails started to bleed. It was comforting. I bit down harder on my thumbnail and bright red blood trickled down my hand.

On the day of my Communion, my mother would not allow me to go to the convent for the breakfast organised by the nuns. I was the only one to be excluded and was delighted.

She was afraid that I would soil my beautiful virgin-white lace dress. It had been made especially for me by my aunt. Auntie Carmel was my father's unmarried sister and she lived with his invalid mother in Harold's Cross, a small village outside Dublin. My mother had painstakingly chosen the white lace and satin lining and my auntie had taken weeks to make it to my mother's specifications. I would sit or stand as she pinned the material. I spent hours being prodded and pricked. Nana would look on and make witty comments.

"Sure, what are ye doing there? It's not her wedding day. It's her bloody Communion," she said in her flat Dublin accent.

My mother looked at her in disgust. My father's family came from what Mammy considered to be a more working-class background and she ignored their banter. However, she respected the old lady in other ways. Often, when my father's cheque had not come on time, we would arrive down at Nana's for a loan. A 'loan' was a wad of money that Nana had under her garter. She would lift her skirts and my brothers and I were told to turn away and Nana would count out what my mother needed. Then, the rest of the money would disappear under her skirt again. She had saved us from many a sticky situation but my mother knew it was wise to keep her mouth shut.

The white dress looked immaculate on the day. My hair had been curled and my veil with its single white rose was simple and endearing. It was a short veil, unusual at the time. I yearned for a long one, like the other girls. But my mother was adamant.

"A long veil will detract from the lace of the dress," she said. And that was that.

As the procession of young white virgins started up the aisle of the church, their long veils flowed in unison and I felt naked with my shorter one. The fact that I towered over the others did not help my feeling of being exposed.

Of course, Mother Joseph commented on the short veil.

"No veil would be long enough to cover up all your sins," she said. "Satan resides in your very soul."

I tried to think of all the bad things I had done, listing them in my head.

I was disobedient to Mammy. I hit one of my brothers but only because he hit me first. I hated the nuns. All of them. Should I love them? I stole some chocolate from Mammy's special sweets' drawer. But I had told her afterwards.

It wasn't a long list but I felt a black mark on my soul. I had visions of walking up to receive the Host and being told to step aside. I could imagine the priest saying to me: "You are a sinner and a whore and I cannot give you the Holy Host."

I felt wretched and sick and looked around to find my mother's face. My father could not come to the communion. He was at sea. I saw my mother sitting there on her own, while all the other couples sat together. I felt a stab of pain in my heart. My brothers were seated at each side of her. One of the nuns pushed me towards the priest.

The priest took the white round Host out of the beautiful silver chalice and placed it on my tongue.

"Under no circumstances are you to chew the Holy Host," we had been told by Mother Patrick. "That would be like chewing the Sacred Heart's body itself. You will swallow it immediately it goes on your tongue. Do not let it touch your lips or teeth, or you will be damned to hell."

I felt like gagging. The Host was so dry that it stuck to my palate. I started to panic. As I was walking back to my seat, I looked at the other children. They seemed to have swallowed Jesus in one go. I remembered Mother Patrick's threats and prised the Host away from my palate, swallowing as if my life depended on it. I glanced around, making sure that no nun was in the vicinity. I had been so busy trying to manoeuvre Jesus himself that two red spots had sprung up on my cheeks. I felt on fire and wanted to drink the holy water font dry. I prayed that the whole thing would be over. A young nun approached me. She was the novice who followed Mother Patrick around.

"Are you feeling alright?" she whispered.

"I'm grand," I said quietly and looked at the cold stone floor of the church.

She went back to Mother Patrick and I dreaded Monday.

Mammy took us to a beautiful restaurant and we had a lovely day. We visited our relatives and shiny new shillings were placed in my white little puffy bag. I wished Daddy was there to see me. I blew him a kiss in his faraway place. I knew he was thinking of me.

I had a lovely ice-cream dessert and imagined that Daddy was sharing it with me. He loved ice-cream. Whenever he came home, the first thing he would do was ask Turlough to go and get a block of HB ice-cream. He would give my brother a shiny two and sixpence coin and my brother would run like the wind to the local shops. Daddy loved vanilla with raspberry ripple and he would smack his lips with enjoyment. It seemed they didn't have ice-cream on board the ship. It was the one thing he craved when he came home.

On Monday, Mother Patrick approached me.

"Of course, always looking for some sort of attention," she said. "Trying to choke on the Holy Host. He didn't want you to swallow him because he knows the Jezebel you are, the black, stinking Jezebel that you are."

The cane strokes came down again and again on my fingers. I sang in my head to the rhythm:

"Holy Host, have mercy on me
I did not mean to be
I did not mean to be
I did not mean to be
BAD BAD BAD BAD."

Mother Joseph stopped, her sweaty forehead shining. I bent my head and dared not touch my hands. My tears fell onto the book we were reading. One tear fell on the word 'almost'.

Daddy is almost home, I remember thinking. But almost is not now. Almost was a long way away. Almost was almost.

CHAPTER 7

NINE
IN THE WARDROBE

I begged my mother to let me stay with my friend Brenda for the weekend. Mammy was apprehensive but agreed. Brenda's father was a good friend of the family and had six children: Brenda, her twin sisters and three brothers. They lived on the north side of town and came regularly to visit. My father played chess with Mr Hawthorn when he was home from sea. Mr Hawthorn's wife would chat gaily in the kitchen with my mother while we children played outside.

Mr Hawthorn always wore short sleeves. I remember gazing at his speckled forearms and fine hairs sprouting in all directions. My daddy had tanned dark arms and I would curl the long dark hair around my fingers.

"Are you plucking a wild chicken?" his voice would boom, and we would laugh together. He would wrap his strong arms around me and I would smell pipe tobacco and the strange places he'd been.

My brothers adored it when he came home. We all drank in his bigness and the whole neighbourhood seemed to join in our gaiety. He would organise volleyball competitions in our back garden and streams of children would come through our house. My poor mother couldn't cope.

"Paddy, don't be asking those kids in today. They're wrecking the place," she would say. But there was a part of her that enjoyed the busyness. Her flushed face and sparkly eyes made me feel happy for her. When Mammy was happy, I was happy.

I was so excited to be going on this adventure. My mother bought new underwear for me. So pretty and with rosebuds on them. I helped her pack them in my candy-striped overnight case. She folded them neatly and told me to be a good girl. She wrapped herself around me and I felt her loneliness. I started feeling guilty that I was so happy.

"Mammy, sure I'll only be gone for the weekend," I said.

"Remember not to eat too much," she replied, "or you will be sick."

We played hide-and-seek all afternoon in their small house. Mr Hawthorn was a scouting leader and always had great stories to tell. He decided to play with us as well.

I chose to hide in a big, dark oak wardrobe upstairs in the attic. It excited yet frightened me. The wardrobe had been left to them by an old aunt, Brenda had said when we were exploring the house, and was so big that they had had to move it up to the attic. They used it to store old coats and jackets and things that they hardly ever used.

I beckoned Mr Hawthorn to join me in the wardrobe. We hid cosily at the back of the oak panels. There were lots of old clothes lined up on big wooden hangers. I liked the smell and felt safe. Mr Hawthorn stood behind

me and wrapped his arms around me. It felt comforting.
I thought about my daddy and how different his
arms were.

"They will never catch us in here," I said and
he agreed. We giggled and I moved closer to him.
The darkness closed in upon us and suddenly
something changed.

"Be quiet," he said.

"But I am not making a sound," I said, confused.
"They won't hear us."

I thought of everyone looking for us. I was delighted
that we had found such a good hiding place.

Mr Hawthorn forced himself on me from behind. I
realised that something was happening but did not
understand what. The pain was so intense that I couldn't
breathe. I was impaled on him and could not move. His
hands were around my waist and he had my arms pinned
down to my sides.

"Don't move," he ordered.
My mind took me away to a beautiful carousel horse
riding around at the fair. My horse was the most beautiful.
He had bright pink and yellow flowers on his golden
mane and he took me away from all the bad places in my
dreams. I don't know how long it lasted.

"You are a big girl now," he said when he had stopped.
Then he started to cry. "May God forgive me," he said.
But would God forgive *me*? But there was only silence
in the darkness.

The wardrobe door opened slightly and in the pencil
of light I saw streaks of blood running down my legs.
I felt no pain but I wondered if this were the blood
of Christ.

He told me to say that I had hurt myself while playing. He left me behind, alone.

"Catch me if you can," I heard him saying to the other children in the distance. My new underwear was around my ankles, streaked red. I thought about the thorns on Jesus's head. I stroked the St Christopher's medal pinned to my vest. He was supposed to protect me. Mammy had been worried about the journey in the car.

"Pray to St Christopher to keep you safe," she had said.

"But Mammy, I will be fine. You are not to worry now," I had said, blowing her a kiss from the car window.

I stepped out of my rosebud pants and threw them into the back of the wardrobe. They disappeared into the darkness. I wanted to follow. Brenda opened the wardrobe door.

"There you are," she exclaimed. "We were looking everywhere for you."

She took my hand and I stepped out into the light.

I asked Mrs Hawthorn to take me home. She could not drive. He would have to take me home.

"Sure, it's only one more night," she said.

I whimpered. She ran a bath for me and closed the bathroom door. Her auburn curls had been newly permed and her hair looked like my mother's. I wanted to touch the goldenness but she stripped me bare and placed me in the bath. She whispered something that sounded like "bitch whore". I began to sing at the top of my voice.

"You are a strange little girl," she said, smiling.

She wrapped a big white towel around me and told me that I had strange dreams. I told her about the carousel horse and we laughed. She told me to be a good little girl and keep my dreams to myself.

We all sat down to dinner. Brenda's noisy brothers and elder twin sisters were shouting at each other. The long dinner table was too big for the living room. This meant that we had to squeeze in very close beside each other. I had made sure that I squeezed in beside my friend and her sister. I enjoyed the noisiness and avoided looking at Mr and Mrs Hawthorn.

He sat at the head of the table and she sat on his right-hand side. She nodded at him to begin carving. He sliced the roast beef with expert hands. I watched the steel blade slicing into the red-brown flesh. He parted his mouth whilst cutting and his yellow teeth opened and shut. I was reminded of a ventriloquist's dummy that I had seen on the television. The dummy's mouth opened and shut and the man spoke through the dummy. I made up conversations in my head whilst he was cutting.

"It's a nice day."

"Let's have a game of hide-and-seek."

"God forgive them for they know not what they do."

I started to laugh and they all wanted to know why. I told the kids that I was making up jokes. We all started telling jokes to each other. I did not want the talking to stop. I wanted it to fill up all the spaces in the already overfull room. I wanted it to lift me off back to my own house and safe bed. Daddy said sound could travel. If it became noisy enough, it would bring me safely home. Sound could travel at the speed of light.

I looked up at the dusty old chandelier. It flickered. But nothing happened.

I hoped that the plate would not bleed too. The big plate of meat was put in front of me. I felt the fork's prongs digging into the solid flesh. Bile came up into my throat. Oh God, not now, I thought. I kept on talking through the whole meal so that I did not have to eat the red slime in front of me.

"You are a very talkative little girl,' said Mrs Hawthorn. Her smile sent shivers down my spine.

Mr Hawthorn ripped the flesh with his knife and fork and pierced each slice before lifting it to his mouth. His eyes glinted under the dusty chandelier. I wanted to carve his heart into neat slices. A song came into my head:

"Take the knife and make it red
Cut his wormy thing until it's dead."

I was frightened by my own thoughts. It was only a dream, Niamh, I told myself. Only a dream.

At dessert I was allowed to have as much ice-cream as I wanted. There were protests among the other kids.

"Why does she get more than us?" they asked.

"Because she's our special guest,"
Mr Hawthorn said.

I dared not look at him but sneaked fleeting glances his way. I saw his long pink tongue searching for the remnants of ice-cream on his spoon. He slurped up his ice-cream and licked his pale lips. My crimson rippled ice-cream started to melt in my bowl. Its creaminess ran down my spoon. I threw up into my glassy bowl. I gagged and retched every morsel of food out of my body.

I wanted it to explode in his face. Everybody jumped up from their seats. They screamed. They gasped in disgust. I threw the glassy bowl and its contents over the table and then stood there and waited. Chaos ensued. Screaming, crying children were running, trying to avoid the mess spilling over the long wooden table. The small room seemed even smaller. The table looked even bigger.

Mr Hawthorn sat there and didn't move. I willed the vomit to go in his direction. Long watery threads nearly reached him but stopped short of his twitching fingers holding on to the wooden ledge of the table. The table was too long for the slimy globules to reach him. I should have thrown up more, I thought. But there was nothing left in my empty body.

"Put that bloody child to bed," he roared.

I screamed, a wolf-like cry coming from the bowels of my abdomen. It was so loud that I thought it came from somewhere else. The children were silenced and the only other sound was the ticking of the faded Mickey Mouse clock in the corner. His big ears flapped in time with my song.

"Ooooooooooooooooooh.   Ooooooooooooooooooh," I wailed.

I was pushed up the stairs by Mrs Hawthorn. The other children were shouting at me.

"You are raving mad," the children shouted. "Daddy's going to slap you."

I begged Brenda to come upstairs with me and she followed. Her mother didn't ask what was wrong. He did not follow us upstairs.

"You can clean up the bloody mess," I heard Mrs Hawthorn say to him.

I was a long way from home. I pictured my mother baking apple pie in our bright yellow kitchen. Mammy help me. Daddy, come home.

I chose the top bunk bed. It was very high and there was no ladder. You had to use a chair to get up on the top bunk and pull yourself up and roll on the bed. We had already played games that afternoon and I knew that a grown-up would have difficulty climbing onto the top bunk. Something deep inside of me told me to sleep there.

"Daddy made the bunk bed but he made it too high," Brenda had explained. "He is not so good at making things."

I got onto the top bunk and threw the chair to the other side of the bedroom. It landed with a crash against the small sink in the left-hand corner of the room. Brenda and I giggled.

"You don't mind that I have the top bunk?" I asked Brenda in the darkness.

"No, not at all. It's nice and cosy up there."

"Goodnight," I said.

"Goodnight. Don't let the bed bugs bite," she said, then added "Daddy's going to come in and read us a story."

I jumped up and hit my head against the cracked ceiling. I followed the long crack with my finger. It had the shape of a long river, like the one I had seen in my book from Daddy. The Amazon, that was it. The Indians fished there with their spears. I got my imaginary spear out to fight the oncoming enemy.

I heard Brenda's soft breathing and asked Angel Gabriel to protect us. But I did not hold out much hope.

My mind began to clear. It felt like the sun had come out after a misty day. I was in the clearing of the jungle waiting for the hunt to begin.

I waited and waited. It seemed such a long, long time. My empty stomach rumbled in the darkness. I whispered to my St Christopher's medal to "bugger off" and tried to rip the cold steel from my chest. But I knew I had to preserve my strength for what was about to take place. Daddy said that I was a warrior like the *fianna*, the Celtic warrior tribes of long ago. His stories echoed in my mind and I braced myself for the battle to come. I sang my plan in my head.

"Warriors of old and warriors of new
Roll like a rock into the coming dew."

The sliver of light shone through as our door opened.

He whispered my name.

"Niamh, are you awake?" he said. "I've come to tell you a story."

I pretended to be asleep. I had rolled against the wall and elongated myself so that I was almost part of it. My nose touched the pretty pink rose-petalled wallpaper. The seam of the wallpaper had a gap. Another job badly done by Mr Hawthorn.

He would have difficulty grabbing me, I thought, and made myself as invisible as possible. I had put the flannel blankets over my head and tucked them at all angles into the small of my back and the back of my legs. My heart was thumping and I felt pulses throughout my body. I saw Mammy ironing in our kitchen as I handed her each article to be ironed. My pleated Sunday skirt was the most difficult and I counted the pink pleats on the ironing board. I saw Daddy handing me a warrior's sword and telling me to fight for the Irish cause.

"I've got something for you."Mister Hawthorn stood beside the bed, his head level with the wooden guardrail. He reached up his skinny arms and tried to grab at me. I wriggled away, like one of St Patrick's snakes. I kicked out and my foot caught him in his face. He shouted something obscure and grabbed a handful of a blanket instead.

"I'm going to get you," he said.

"John, don't forget to…" Mrs Hawthorn was shouting something at him from downstairs.

I heard him cursing in the darkness and punching the steel bar of the bunk bed. I felt the vibrations in the pit of my stomach. He whispered to his daughter and I did not listen. He left the room briefly.

I had chosen the top bunk. I was safe. I had fought the enemy. Daddy would be so proud of me. I remember breathing through the blanket and hoping that I was invisible enough.

I prayed to God to keep Brenda safe, but then again, He had not kept me safe in the wardrobe.
"Please God, I will be a good little girl forever and ever and I will do anything you say," I pleaded.

I was lucky. I heard strange things that night. My little friend was not so lucky. Muffled sounds and odd smells permeated the room. I wanted to help her but I chose not to hear. I wrapped myself further into the blankets and sang songs that I hoped would reach her. I felt I had betrayed her. I should have been the one on the bottom bunk. The night was long for both of us. Finally the Amazon jungle and its sounds brought me into their world. I welcomed the river's edge and fell into a dazed sleep.

My dreams were long and troubled that night. Sunlight peeped through the curtains to say hello. I leaned over the edge of my bed and looked down at Brenda.

"Good morning Brenda," I said.

Brenda was very quiet and she looked at me with such sadness. I didn't know what to say. Had I dreamed hearing those noises?

"Don't come here again," she said." Daddy loves me."

"Of course he does," I replied.

I climbed down to join her and caught her little button nose between my two fingers. I pulled it gently. Her freckles reminded me of sprinkles on ice-cream cones. I reached out for her but she refused. She stepped out of her pyjamas and quickly dressed. I dressed hurriedly as well.

I closed the bedroom door behind me as we began to walk downstairs for breakfast. I caught a glimpse of her tattered teddy bear, Eddy. He sat on her bed. He couldn't help her either. His beady black eyes showed no expression. I ran back and flung him on the floor.

"Bad Eddy, you could have done something," I said.

When it was time to go home, I begged that my friend should come too. Mrs Hawthorn agreed and waved us off. She buttoned my coat as it was cold outside.

"Be a good girl," she said.

"I will," I said chirpily. I had just had a bad dream,

I told myself. I had had a great time. The boys ran after the car and I waved goodbye until they became specks in the distance. I sat into the brown leather back seat. It felt clammy and cold. I placed my hands under my bottom. They would be safe there.

He had insisted that I sit in the front seat beside him. But Brenda had screamed so much that his wife told him that I should sit in the back. Something told me that I had been saved yet again. The forty-five minute journey home seemed a long way to my nine-year-old self.

He had one hand on the steering wheel, which I thought was very odd. His other hand had disappeared under my friend's skirt. She said nothing and I did not understand where his hand could possibly be. I knew that it had something to do with darkness. But the sun shone brightly outside and my bad dreams only took place at night. I realised then that we were not safe in daylight either.

Every now and again I felt his eyes on me. His face had become bright red and I saw the veins in his eyes turning a deeper colour. They looked like some of the marbles from my collection. I counted out my coloured marbles in my head. The blue-green one was my favourite. I had won it from my big brother. I started to sing "It's a long way to Tipperary" and my voice got louder and louder. My little friend did not join in. I wanted her to sing with me. Brenda, sing with me, sing with me, I thought. We would sing and sing until we disappeared.

"Shut up back there or I'll come and get you," he said.

He stopped the car. My song has saved us, I thought. He is going to disappear. But he only wanted to go to the toilet.

"We're making a toilet stop. Come on girls, follow me."

He stepped out of the car. We were parked at the side of the road and there was thick woodland in the distance.

"Are you coming then?" he asked.

"I am feeling sick," I said, making a convincing gagging sound. He went without me and his daughter started to follow.

"Don't go with him," I said, grabbing her hand. She pushed me away and didn't look back at me.

My heart raced and I wanted to run after them. I needed to go to the toilet too, but something told me to stay in the car. I remember counting the trees and hoping that it would rain. But it was a beautiful sunny day. Lots of cars passed us on the roadside. I wanted them to stop and ask what was happening. But nobody did and I stuck out my tongue out at all of them until my jaw was tired and my mouth dry. The traffic became a blur of colour as I sat back and waited. I thought of Daddy on his ship. I felt warm and sticky and my head swirled with all the bad dreams. I stuck to the leather seat and heard sucking sounds as I moved from one buttock to the other. I made a game of it.

"Bottoms sticking to the seat
Chocolate buttons good enough to eat."

When they both emerged from the greenness, the wind seemed to be pushing them toward me. I knew the trees did not want them there. The trees were good trees. My little friend avoided my eyes. A tear had escaped from the corner of her eye. I wanted to catch it for her but knew that I couldn't. I blew her a kiss. She did not respond.

We drove off and I did not sing again. The back of her head did not move for the rest of the journey. I wrapped a strand of her auburn hair around my finger and hoped she knew I was there for her.

My mother greeted us at the door. Her newly permed hair was tight against her head. I ran to her and wrapped myself around her. I would not let go. She was delighted that I had missed her, I could tell.

"Did you have a nice time?" she asked.

"Yes, Mammy, the best."

"So you didn't miss me at all?"

"I did, Mammy, I did," I said.

Mr Hawthorn confirmed that I had had a great time. He said that I was welcome to come again.

"But we are not friends anymore," Brenda exclaimed. "I don't want her to come."

I still had my head in my mother's ample bosom. It felt like a soft pillow and I closed my eyes. I was safe.

"That did you good," my mother said, as we waved them off "Maybe you can go another time. You are becoming a big girl."

"No, Mammy, I am your little girl. I will always be your little girl."

I said it with such conviction that my mother smiled triumphantly.

"Yes you are and always will be," she said and we went hand in hand into the kitchen.

"Mammy's little girl," my brothers chimed. "Mammy's little girl . . ."

They stuck their tongues out at me and I started to cry. I couldn't stop. I threw up on the clean kitchen floor.

"What were they feeding you there?" Mammy asked, exasperated

I was sat down to a big bowl of Irish stew. I did not know whether to eat it or not. I waited for Mammy's reaction. She seemed to want me to eat, so I ate.

My tummy and bottom ached. I dared not say anything. It was only a bad dream. Mammy was too busy looking after us. But I had a feeling that my home was not as safe as it should be. It was a confusing place to be. Safe was only a word and words meant nothing to me now. But it was the only safe I knew and I held onto that.

I had difficulty hearing from that day on. I listened to things but I did not hear. I told no one about what had happened. My mother was struggling bringing up three children and my father was at sea. It was easier to forget. And I couldn't even remember anyway. I no longer believed what I heard. I felt guilty because I had begged my mother to let me go to Brenda's. She would only have said, "I told you so". I could not hurt her further by sharing what had happened. I had disappointed her enough by being me. I chose to remain a little girl inside, innocent, naive. It was easier that way. After all, God had saved me on the ride home, hadn't he and I had promised to be a good little girl? And I was. I had invited Mr Hawthorn into the wardrobe. I could pretend it was just another dream.

I had bad dreams about being in a very dark place and nobody being able to rescue me. I woke up and the silence of the night did not help. I had to go to school and endure another nightmare. The nightmares in my sleep were better than the nightmares of the day.

CHAPTER 8

NINE AND A HALF
THE BLOOD OF CHRIST

At first my mother thought I had eaten too many chocolate Easter eggs. My brothers and I had scoffed so many after Sunday Mass. Once our new outfits had been put away, we proceeded to unravel the coloured foil from every Easter egg and take large bites from each one. I felt quite nauseous, which was nothing new for me.

My mother's friend happened to come by with her children that day. I cried out in the bathroom. I had seen blood like this before but couldn't remember exactly where. I did not want to go into that dark place in my mind. I howled. The fear was unbearable. My blood-streaked legs brought unwelcome memories.

I thought I was imagining the crimson stains on my white underpants. I dared not touch them. My mother came to see what was going on. She let out a scream and ran to her friend. She was inconsolable.

I listened to her gasps and whispers from the landing. Her friend comforted her and her tears pulled at my heart. I crouched further into the darkness on the landing and the new burgundy red carpet felt soft and cushiony below my toes. But the colour disgusted me. I was on the Red Sea and I was bloodied and dirty.

My mother caught a glimpse of me on the stairs but avoided my gaze. It made me feel even worse. I wanted her to wrap me in her arms and comfort me. But I sat there instead, waiting for her to calm down while her friend made her a cup of tea.

My brothers continued scoffing their Easter eggs. I felt like the bitch whore all over again.

"But I have been a good girl," I cried out to baby Jesus.

"All girls have to bleed for the sins of Jesus," my mother told me later. "Even Mother Mary herself paid for the sins of her son. Every month we have to bleed for the sins of the world."

I remember thinking that I had already bled once before. Was I to bleed for every man? I wondered if Daddy would still love me when he came home from sea. My tummy ached and I wiped the chocolate from my mouth. Its sweet taste comforted and disgusted me. I threw the remnants of my chocolate eggs down the stairs. My brothers fought for the spoils. I watched them greedily picking up the small pieces and I cried out.

My mother put me to bed with a hot water bottle. I felt her discomfort. She said we could pick out a nice calendar the next day to mark my monthly arrival. She would have to watch me now like a hawk, she said.

"What do you mean?" I asked.

"You are a big girl now," she replied.

That night, I dreamt of chocolate Easter eggs and Jesus on the cross. I fed him chocolate with a long spear. His wounds opened and melting chocolate steamed out of his hands and feet. I preferred a chocolate Jesus and I asked him to forgive me for being such a bloody girl. He said nothing. He just smiled.

Mammy said she would buy me a special calendar. I chose a Holly Hobby one with sweet little girls in sweet little dresses. My mother warned me that I would receive 'a message' every month. If I did not, it would be very dangerous. I did not understand.

"Do not talk to any strange men," she said.

I told her I wouldn't. She said that we had to keep this a secret. I was terrified.

The next stop was the chemist. Whispering, we picked out a pretty toiletry bag for my sanitary pads.

I felt I was in the middle of some great conspiracy but I was not sure if I was party to it or not. I saw a young girl of my age with her mother, holding her hand, laughing and buying toothpaste. I longed to buy toothpaste as well. I wanted to be like her. I was also a little girl. My mother went to the cash desk with our secret purchases. She told me to wait at the door of the shop whilst she was paying. I hung my head in shame. I felt that the whole world was turning away from me.

My mother turned around and smiled at me. Her moist eyes confused me. Had I done something wrong? Did the nuns tell her something that I should know about? Was she so disappointed in me?

My brain was on overload. I had to keep on moving to the side as people tried to get past me to walk out the narrow door. They stared at me and I became convinced that they knew my secret too. It didn't dawn on me to think that this tall slender white-haired girl was being admired. I hung my head further until I felt my neck was detaching from my body. Mammy took me by the hand and told me to put my shoulders back and my head up high. I was already taller than her and it felt strange to hold her hand. We walked out into the busy street and I caught my reflection in the shop window.

"Don't be looking at yourself in the window," she said. "Vanity is an awful thing."

She proceeded to pull me away from anything that reflected our images. I noticed that she avoided any contact with her own reflection too. It was hard though, considering the whole street was full of shop windows.

Mammy made me wear two vests.

"They'll keep your breasts nice and flat," she said. "You need to look like a normal nine-year-old. Nobody should get a period so young."

This only confirmed how different I was. Mammy went to the nuns to explain the situation. I was allowed to leave the classroom more often to go to the toilet. My big colourful toiletry bag did not help things. The problem was that it was too nice. It had yellow and white marigolds on it. It was very pretty. My mother thought this would compensate for its contents. All the children would ask me where I was going. I was sworn to secrecy because if the parents found out that their little girls knew about that sort of thing, I would be in big trouble. Only Mammy and I and the nuns could know, she said. The other children were too young to know about it.

"But Mammy, I am a little girl too," I said.

"Niamh, you are caught between worlds, between a little girl and a young woman."

But the words 'too young' were all I heard.

"Please may I be excused?" I asked, rising from my desk.

Sister McAletta looked at me with disdain but nodded.

"Where are you going?" the children would whisper.

"Where nobody can see me," I sometimes replied.

My frequent unexplained exits distanced me further from my classmates. It must have been very strange to see me walking out the door with a huge bright toiletry bag under my arm. The nun forbade the children to look into the bag. If they did, she said, they would be expelled immediately. The toiletry bag became a great fear factor in our young lives. In the end they were too terrified to know what the contents of my special bag actually were, just as I was terrified about having to use them. It gave Mother Joseph another excuse to taunt me.

"Well Niamh, the whore of Babylon, where are you going with your whore's bag?" she would say.

One time, I didn't go to the toilet for the whole day and the bright red patch on my uniform became another reason for ridicule.

"Whores always wear a sign," she said. "God has chosen you to walk at the side of Satan."

The other young girls were scared that they too would get a sign and avoided me.

I seemed to follow my toiletry bag instead of the other way round. In my mind, this huge bag dominated my whole life. I hated every month that my curse visited me. These huge white things had to be placed between my legs. I loathed the whole idea and I threw up on the cold polished floors. My retching echoed through the old school corridors. The parquet floor and its diagonal pattern looked up at me. We were old friends. It was almost comforting to be able to vomit in the same place.

"Here we go again," I said to the floor and wiped up the vomit with my sanitary towels. I found them quite funny sometimes and slid over the polished floors with one on each foot. I took off one pair of underpants and wiped up the remnants of my breakfast. I always wore two pairs of underpants. My mother had theories about that which I did not quite understand. I threw the soiled cotton out of the convent window. They landed on a tree. I saw them swaying on the branches and eventually blow away and disappear into the distance. I didn't care. I giggled. I hoped they'd land on an unsuspecting novice nun.

Novice nuns were locked up in that part of the convent garden. They would appear and then disappear just as quickly. We often wondered where they went. My underpants had disappeared to that place too and that consoled me.

I never really smelled properly after that.

The acid smell of vomit and the metallic smell of blood had tainted me. I was even afraid to smell the flowers. When I received presents of flowers, I would say how beautiful they smelled. I was a master at using the words. But no smell could penetrate my senses. Perfume all smelled the same. The fear of smelling was too great. I feared that I would also contaminate the beauty of the smell itself.

The more my breasts grew the more I felt rejected by my mother. She told me that she found breasts disgusting.

"Put them away", she would pipe up.

Where could I put them? Where?

I was a member of a swimming club for a while but never came first in a competition.

"You'll never win anyway, so it's best you don't go at all, Niamh," she said but I knew she hated seeing my breasts on display inside a swimsuit and comparing all those skinny girls with me.

"Why are they so thin? What do their mothers give them to eat?" Mammy would whisper to me while we were in the changing room.

But I loved to swim. I had won a few medals but never a cup. It was the cup that was the most important. A medal was for a runner-up. Mammy made me leave the swimming club.

My Irish dance classes did not last long either. I dressed up in a beautiful striped pinafore and embroidered blouse to enter a dance competition but I didn't win the cup.

"The trouble with you, Niamh, is that you have no rhythm," she said. "It'll be best that you leave. You'll only end up hurt when you keep on losing."

But I loved to dance. Although Mammy knew best so I never sang when Mammy was around.

Daddy enrolled me in the Brownies. My brothers were already in the sea-scouts.

"Now, Padraicin, let her go out and meet some other children," Daddy said.

Daddy went away. I lasted two meetings at the Brownies.

"The children are not friendly there. Are they?" Mammy stated to me.

I never went again. I shoved my little brown uniform and yellow tie and toggle into the wardrobe. I would have loved to have had the pretty badges that the other girls had. I closed the wardrobe quickly and my uniform disappeared forever.

CHAPTER 9

TEN
RONKA

The Reverend Mother came into our classroom. She only came in on very special occasions. Behind her walked a tall chocolate brown girl. The nun told us that she would be coming to our school for a while. She was staying with an aunt in the area. Apparently, her mother had been Irish and had moved to Nigeria and married an African but then she had died of a fever. Her husband had promised to send their daughter to her old school. The nun went on and on but I was not listening. I was fascinated by this brown vision coming into our lives. The nun told her to take a desk and place it where she liked. Her name was Ronka.

Ronka hesitated and most of the girls bent their heads. They did not want this strange being sitting beside them. But we caught each other's eye and she moved towards me. She placed her desk beside mine. I glanced at her teardrops forming little pools on her fleshy pink lips. I reached out for her hand under our desks. She took it gladly and squeezed it gently. I caught a glimpse of a salmon pink palm through our entwined fingers. Ronka smelled of faraway places. Places I had been in my dreams. The soft texture of her palm and the gentle strength of her fingers gave me an overwhelming feeling of warmth and safety.

Sister McAletta cackled.

"Well, Niamh, never let it be said that you are the only oddball in the class."

Ronka looked at me. She smiled and her pearly white teeth dazzled me. Sister McAletta smashed her bamboo cane between us and our hands fell to our sides.

"I will write to my father about this situation," Ronka said. Her accent was soft and lilting. "It is a very bad situation indeed. The nuns in my country do not use such things. Please reserve your anger for those who are deserving."

Sister McAletta held on to her desk in shock, her knuckles white and fingers spidery. Her reddened face was bloated and sweaty. She left the classroom.

The whole class gasped and I was speechless. Ronka immediately became my friend.

"This is a very strange country indeed," she said.

She touched one of my locks of blond hair and wound it round her finger, watching the coiled spring bounce when she let it go. I held onto her hand and never wanted to let go.

Sister McAletta left us alone and ignored us. Her silence was the most powerful thing of all. I knew that Ronka was an important person.

We were inseparable. I would wait for her at the school gates and take her to her bus stop every afternoon. She had two older cousins at our school but it was clear that they did not like the idea of her staying with them. It seemed that their mother was her mother's sister and she was staying with them until her father sent for her. Her father was an officer in the Nigerian army and her two older brothers were also in Nigeria.

I began to speak in her lilting accent at home and would pipe up with things like, "No, I do not appreciate you annoying me. It is better for you to play outside in the sunshine."

My brothers would laugh hysterically. Ronka would sing me songs of her country and I would hum them to myself later in the darkness of my room.

We would make up songs together. The lyrics spoke about sunshine and had lots of foreign words.

"The medicine man will come to bless the village
The medicine man will make many strong sons
The medicine man will bring good harvests
The medicine man will marry my daughter soon."

Ronka was further on than us in her education. She was clever. The nuns could not break her spirit and I had a very peaceful time in her company. At break time, we would sneak off and she would tell me stories of her faraway land. She missed home and I would listen to her longings of going back.

"You are coming back with me and you will have many servants and riches," she said.

"Can I be a princess too?"

"Of course you can. Your golden hair will have many men knocking on your door. Your father will have to ask for many animals for you."

"What kind of animals?"

"Cows and goats."

"Can I keep them in the house?"

"Yes, we will make a special place for them."

"Will you come and visit me every day?"

"Of course I will and I will bring many gifts to you and your family."

"Can I eat as much as I like there?"

"Of course you can. I will make you very special dishes known only in my country."

"Will I like them? Will I be sick?"

"Nobody gets sick from Ronka's special cooking. You will grow fat and old and happy."

"I'm not allowed to be fat but maybe Mammy will let me because it's another country."

Ronka smiled and pinched my cheeks and we laughed until our sides burst.

We would have imaginary afternoon tea every day in the playground or I would bathe in the local river whilst she protected me against the crocodiles. When the sun shone, she took off her knee socks and shoes and placed her long graceful toes in the earth. I was too terrified to do likewise. But I watched her elegant toes wiggle in the mossy earth. She would quickly replace her shoes and socks when a nun started approaching. The nuns kept their distance but watched us closely. Ronka said that it was like a prison there in that school.

"In my country, we can walk barefoot and nobody cares," she said. "The nuns accept us as we are and are kind to us."

I could not imagine my black-robed enemies being kind to me and an ache engulfed me.

"Are whores allowed to live in your country?"

Ronka was shocked. "That is only a word, Niamh, and you are much more than words."

It was the nicest thing anybody had ever said to me.

She lifted my hand and began to read my palm.

"Niamh, you will live a long, happy life and have many children."

I took her palm in my hand and traced the light brown lines. "Ronka, you will marry a white prince," I told her. She was not pleased.

"Niamh, I am destined to marry a black prince with dark curling hair," she said.

So, I changed my predictions and we laughed.

She was so easy to love. I knew she loved me too. She would sometimes take one of my flaxen curls in her hand and touch it and smell it. She said it reminded her of the golden corn that grew in her village. She hated having her hair tied back so tightly. Her aunt tried to make it as European as possible. But inevitably, by the end of the day, little black curls would escape from her ponytail. I loved to see them peeping out and falling on her brow. I wanted to feel their texture but was afraid. My touch might make something happen to her. The nuns had instilled in me the belief that I was evil. I was terrified to touch this beautiful friend of mine sometimes. Other times, I would cling on to her hand but would have to let go when the black brigade started to approach. They kept an eye on us and when they thought that we were spending too much time together, they would separate us. It was as if they knew that I was stronger when I was with Ronka. My beatings were less frequent then, too.

I was so happy. My mother saw that I was looking well and worried that I was getting fat. I started answering her back. I demanded food when I was hungry. I was getting stronger and Mammy didn't like it at all. I rocked the boat in the whole household.

"What has got into you?" she said. "You are getting too cheeky."

One day, I waited at the school and Ronka did not show up. The big school bell rang for the third time. I had to go in. I sat down and looked at her empty place.

Sister McAletta had an announcement to make.

"Ronka has been called back by her father," she said. "She has gone back to Nigeria."-

Sister McAletta looked for my reaction. But her triumph soon turned to disappointment. I purposely blanked out all emotion. I felt numb on the inside.

At home I cried for hours. My mother could not console me.

"It's for the best," she said. "Ronka could not stay here forever."

"She could, she could," I said. "She is my friend. She is my friend. I was to go and live with her and have cows and goats." I got into such a state that I couldn't breathe. My mother didn't know what to do.

A photo was left in the letterbox by Ronka's aunt. It was a photo of my friend with her cousin and uncle. I put it under my pillow and spoke to her every night. I stopped eating and refused to get out of bed. My mother sent for the doctor. She liked this well-to-do, unmarried, Protestant.

The doctor examined me and parted my pink flannel pyjama top. Her cold steel stethoscope shocked my feverish skin. I was burning all over. I protested. But she was a no-nonsense type of woman. She took the photo of Ronka out from under my pillow and handed it to my mother. I saw it disappear behind my mother's back. I screamed and reached out but the doctor shook me roughly.

"Niamh, that's enough. Enough now," she said. "You don't want to worry your mother anymore, do you?"

"Now, Mrs O' Broin, it's for you to fatten that young girl up!" she said.

I watched my mother's jaw drop open in horror.

"Give her anything she wants, so long as she eats."

I asked for French nougat. It came in such a pretty box and each piece was wrapped in silver foil. My mother fed me the nougat from her hand. She felt uncomfortable giving it to me.

"God, I hope you don't end up like that huge Jewess across the park," she said. "She can't walk she's so fat," she said.

I spat out the nougat when she was not looking and wrapped it in the discarded foils. I placed them under the bed. I would never grow fat, old and happy now.

The next day the children taunted me about my chocolate friend being gone. I pushed one girl and she flew against the wall. The nun's cane came down on me like a lightning rod. I hoped God would take me. I prayed again that the devil might take me. But even he didn't want me. I stood bowed and broken. The sting of the cane swipes on my hands consoled me. I blew on my hands and whilst doing so blew a kiss to Ronka, wherever she was.

I never heard from her again. Her chocolate presence faded from my mind and life went on.

Many years later my mother let slip that Ronka had

married an officer in the Nigerian army. It is possible I did receive letters but was not given them. My post had been intercepted my whole life. At that stage I did not care.

I remember making a grey felt mouse in sewing class. The whole class had to make the same mouse from the same pattern. But mine was different. Thirty-eight grey mice were lined up together on the long wooden workbench while mine was put to the side. The nun brought her silver ruler down on my knuckles and called me a Jezebel. My mouse was thrown at me and landed on her desk. The class giggled at the sight of the crooked creature flying through the air. It knocked down the chalk box and the chalk sticks scattered to the floor. I was fascinated by the white flakes on the wooden floor. I wanted to touch the whiteness and spread it on my face and let it make me invisible. I started to laugh and my flaxen curls were pulled until my scalp turned crimson. The more the nun pulled, the more I laughed. I did not feel pain any more. I was in my invisible world. I reached out to touch the whiteness on the floor. The ruler smashed down on my outstretched fingers.

I never really touched things after that.

I stood on the precipice of insanity and felt the only way to stop myself toppling over, into the abyss was by shutting myself off, protecting my senses. My sight, hearing, smell had all been impaired and distorted and now it was the turn of touch. I'd not trust my hands or fingers any more. I loved beautiful things. I would watch people stroking dress material in the stores and back away. I began to fear the things I loved, believing I would contaminate them in some way. I slid in and out of black moods and sang to myself to dull the pain.

And still we waited for Daddy to come home. At that time, a seaman could be gone for nine months of the year. When we were naughty, my mother's cries of "Wait until your father gets home," fell on deaf ears.

But when he did come home, it was a joyous occasion. And just as we had got used to his presence, he would have to leave again. It added to my confusion and turmoil. It was traumatic for me and for my brothers. Mammy suffered greatly as well.

One time, the longest time ever, he had been gone for a year and a half. I came home from school one day to see a bearded stranger sitting at the kitchen table. My mother said that it was my father, but I couldn't recognize him. I went over and kissed his prickly beard. Sure, the man smelled like Daddy, but my sense of smell could not be trusted so I did not know if my truth was the truth at all. I longed to hug my father, but shied away from this bearded man invading my space. He reached out to me and I became hysterical. My mother pushed me into his arms and I froze. His song calmed me down. It was our special song. Only then did I snuggle into him. But still I felt the pain because I was already thinking about when he would leave again. I never felt comfortable in men's company. I always expected them to leave me one day.

CHAPTER 10

ELEVEN
SLAPPED BY THE BISHOP

"This outfit will stand out from all the others," my mother said. We were standing in an exclusive shop in Grafton Street, in Dublin. She had chosen a sky-blue twin set that had a fine sycamore-pink stripe through it. The cardigan had pearly pink buttons and the skirt fell to the knees. My mother chose a silk pink shirt to go under the cardigan and "*la piece de résistance*", as the shop assistant said, was the beret, which had the most beautiful big pom-pom I had ever seen.

"She looks like a model," exclaimed the assistant.

"Mammy, it's for my confirmation," I protested. "All the people will be looking at me."

"Of course they will," she replied. "You want to look different."

She placed the beret at such a steep angle that I was afraid to move in case it fell off. My mother fussed and patted until it was perfect.

"You can eat Mammy's crackers for the next two weeks until your tummy gets flatter," she said.
She patted my little bulge, which it seemed had interfered with the perfect picture. I thought of bearing my teeth down on the horrible dark brown crackers. I felt like pulling the pink pom-pom off my head. I wanted to rip the whole outfit off and run through the shop squealing like a pig.

I looked at my stomach and it grew to such proportions that I felt sick and disappointed. I decided to hold it in more and more. My face turned slightly pink as I caught my reflection in the long gold-framed mirror.

"Is it not time that the young madam wore a little brassiere?" the shop assistant asked my mother.

My mother looked at me intently.

"No, we will wait another little while," she said. "Have you a very tight undergarment with seams in the front? It will hold them down a little longer."

My mother stared at my chest and I felt guilty. I wanted to go home. My mind filled with thoughts of Sister McAletta staring at me. I sang to myself:

"Breasts are not the best
Tear the pom-pom and pink vest."

I dreaded the thought of my breasts being imprisoned tighter. I relished the thought of freedom in my nightdress each evening. I dared not look down at these things of contention. My mother could not cope with the idea of them developing until she thought that the time was right. She had to stop them in whatever way she could. It was my fault I had become womanly so early and I did my best to help Mammy in her mission.

I wanted to look ordinary like the rest of the convent girls. I wanted a pill-box hat on my head and a heavy woollen suit in brown or grey. I wanted heavy brown leather laced-up shoes. I did not want to stand out from the crowd. I didn't want the other mothers whispering and laughing when we walked into the church.

Sister McAletta had told us that the bishop would slap us on the face if we did not know our catechism.

"He might even give *you* an extra slap," she had said to me. "I'll inform him of your badness."

I couldn't sleep for weeks in advance and the thought of being slapped in the church in front of everybody was so frightening that I prayed I would die before the day came. But my prayers were not answered and Mammy, my brothers and I headed down to the church on the big day.

Mother Joseph saw me approaching.

"Should have known that you would be dressed like a Parisian whore," she hissed in my ear when my mother was out of hearing distance. She then proceeded to bash my beret into shape so that it would sit straight up on my head. Unfortunately, it looked more like a jelly that had sunk in the middle. When the pom-pom refused to go anywhere, she beat the top of my head with her clenched fists.

"Niamh, I told you not to touch your beret," my mother said when she saw the state of my beautiful hat. "Now I will have to fix it again." She proceeded to place my beret at the specific angle that was so important to her.

I was relieved when the time came to join the other girls and local boys in a procession into the church. I looked back and saw Mother Joseph and my mother glaring at me. I felt at that moment that they were conspiring together to make me feel miserable. Both expected something that I could not give them.

Thirty-eight grey girls, quiet as mice, walked in front of me and I joined them at the back. The two Marys were in front of me and elbowed each other and giggled. I longed to have a dark brown suit. I was the one felt mouse that stood out from the whole group. I looked down at my perfectly flat chest and perfectly flat tummy. I observed my long mahogany brown legs with the cerise pink pumps. My mother had been determined that I would have brown legs on my big day. This time my mother had forced me to be different. Normally, I managed to do that perfectly well all on my own.

"You will have brown legs on your day," she had said. "There's nothing worse than milk bottle legs."

She had me seated in the part of the garden that trapped the most rays of sun. It was mid-May, I remember, and I sat for hours reading my book. My legs were positioned on a backless chair so that they would get maximum exposure. When it was time for my back legs to be exposed to the sun, I had to turn around and stand for what seemed like hours. I read my book and stood until otherwise instructed. I was not to talk in case the neighbours heard me and wanted to talk over the back wall.

Now and again Mammy would sneak out the back door and look at the results. I felt like the Sunday roast being prodded at and left to season for another while. But I didn't care. I was engrossed in my book and had peace and quiet. My mother had placed a lot of white sheets on the washing line so that nobody could view me from their back gardens. I liked the idea that nobody could see me and standing for a few hours was not a chore for me. My punishment had an upside after all.

Mammy was very proud of the result. Her secret ingredients of olive oil and iodine mixed in a bottle seemed to have done the job. I smiled inwardly as I spotted a small streak on my left kneecap. Imperfection had reared its ugly head.

"A perfect day in an imperfect world," I sang to myself. It gave me solace and I made a note to myself not to draw Mammy's attention to the streaky brown spot on my knee.

I walked tall and elegantly into the church. I happened to be the last of the girls marching up the aisle. I felt all eyes were on me and I wanted to roll up in a ball. But I knew I had to do Mammy proud and I was determined not to let the family down.

When I saw a sea of black at the front of the church, I exaggerated my swagger. I might as well be punished for something decent when I go back to school, I thought. I walked slowly past the black penguin brigade. I just felt their hatred boring into my back. I wished that Daddy was here, but he could not make it home. I saw my brothers and mother. My mother was so proud and gave me a slight nod of acknowledgement. She motioned for me to hold my stomach in and straighten up and I obeyed.

The archbishop wore the most beautiful robes and they glistened in the light of the heavy crystal chandeliers. A group of priests walked down the aisle, followed by the Archbishop and an entourage of red and white altar boys. The children watched on in awe and now and again a whimper would escape.

Those who were being confirmed were seated in the front of the church with the girls on one side and the boys on the other. We were a pool of browns, greys and dark blues. My sky-blue and cerise pink outfit stood out like a red nose on a clown. I knew my pink pom-pom towered over the other heads.

I prayed that the archbishop would be nice to me and not slap me to death as the nuns had suggested he might.

"He will slap the evil out of you and then you will have to kiss his big green ring," they had said.

I scanned his hands and saw the huge green ring on his finger. The light caught it, turning it into a pyramid of light that led my way. I took a deep breath and waited for my turn. He went to each child, asking a question before he gave them a slight tap on the cheek and they kissed his ring. It seemed simple enough and I sat further into my seat with relief.

The time came for Mary, who was next to me, to be confirmed. She answered his question and I saw his hand brush her cheek. She reverently kissed his ring and he moved on to me. I saw him staring at my pom-pom and I thought a slight grin emerged from his withered old face.

Oh no, he is going to call me a Parisian whore, I thought, panicked. He said something to me but I could not understand. He leaned closer to me.

"My child, what is the Trinity?" I heard him say, but his words went right over the top of my head. I thought he was enquiring about my hat. Or was he speaking another language? French maybe?

Silence enveloped the church. He took my hand and I held it to me and would not let it go.

"Father forgive me for I know not what I do," I said. He smiled and tapped me on the cheek and I grabbed his hand again as if it were my only salvation from this madness. I kissed his ring and the cold glass tasted like a big green gobstopper, one of those huge round sweets that barely fitted into your mouth. I almost sucked the ring with relief but decided not to. He placed his hand on my pom-pom and gave me an extra blessing and whispered something into my ear. This time, I thought I understood what he had said and smiled to myself.

After the ceremony, we all stood outside the church with our families. Mary approached me and said that the bishop seemed to really like me.

"Ye got an extra blessing," she said.

We laughed and I moved away. I could only think of the big feast ahead. Mammy had said that I could eat as much as I liked now that the big occasion was over. My stomach rumbled in anticipation. I imagined diving into a giant sorbet ice-cream. I was so relieved it was all over that I was near-hysterical. I ran around the church grounds with the other girls whilst the parents chatted merrily to each other.

A black shadow approached us. It was Sister McAletta.

"Well, typical you, you made a show of the whole school with your conduct in the church. You were a disgrace," she said.

I turned and looked at her.

"No, I wasn't," I said. "The archbishop told me that I was an extraordinary girl. He whispered that to me. I am an extraordinary girl. You can ask him yourself."

She was taken aback and as my mother approached she slid back into the shadows.

"Time to go to the restaurant," my mother said as she fixed my beret. Sister McAletta had again tried to straighten it into some form of decency.

I walked away with my family, leaving a lot of nudging mothers and gossiping nuns behind. I didn't care. I knew what the archbishop had said to me. But I felt apprehensive and started to doubt his words. My mother was very proud of me nonetheless.

"Did you see how he put his hand on your head?" she gushed. "I told you that your outfit was beautiful. He gave you an extra blessing because you are special." I wanted to correct my mother and tell her that he was only trying to calm me down but decided to go with her version of the events. After all, I was *une fille extraordinaire*. He *had* spoken to me in French.

Years later I realised he must have been making a joke at the nuns' expense. I think they must have commented on my outfit in his presence and that he had found it all quite comical and had spoken French to me. I will never forget his kindly old face.

When I went back to school on the Monday, the nuns seemed to hate me even more. They were in a jealous rage. At least six of them surrounded me and demanded to know what the archbishop had said.

"Nobody gets an extra blessing and certainly not the whore of Babylon!" they whispered to each other behind my back.

"You needed the extra blessing because you are so evil," they said to my face.

By that stage, I was not impressed. I had begun to realise that not everything they said was true. I became cheekier in my answers.

"No, that's not true," I said. "In France, they get two blessings. After all, I am the Parisian whore."

They had no response and stormed off into the grey morning sun. I felt triumphant but knew the feeling would not last.

The cane was brought out and smashed down on me again and again but, in time, faced with my constant defiance they began to relent. I no longer reacted the way they wanted me to. Even the class joined in my merriment. They would giggle at my cheeky answers and the nun in question would go crazy. In the last year of primary school, I almost became popular. It was as if the whole class was relieved that they were no longer forced to watch my daily abuse. However, no one escaped the nuns' wrath.

I knew that after the summer I would be going to secondary school so, in my last week, I gave them a run for their money. Despite all their efforts, I was a bright, intelligent girl with an exceptional talent for words. They could not beat that out of me.

It was my home situation that was hardest to endure. My mother's stifling control began to wear me out. At times her resolve was stronger than the nuns'. Try as she might to prevent the march of time, she could not prevent her baby growing into a young woman before her eyes. I had my moments of rebellion but always ended up giving in to her demands. I didn't want to hurt her. I just wanted to make her happy. I didn't realise that pleasing my mother was not a fit task for a young girl, yet it became my preoccupation.

Grandmammy came to the house regularly. She was Mammy's mother. Her fragile and unkempt appearance was always a problem with Mammy. Grandmammy would arrive at the house, smelling funny and often wearing two odd shoes.

"Mammy, you didn't come up the road in that state!" Mammy protested. She would then look out the window making sure that nobody had seen her mother coming into our house.

Grandmammy had a very large brown basket with all bits and pieces in it. We called it her 'Mary Poppins' bag and she would produce all sorts of food or beverages from it.

"Now, gather around, my little birdies, and see what your Grandmammy has for you," she slurred.

My brothers and I would wait excitedly to see what was going to be taken out of the basket. Sometimes, we would get a crisp chicken leg each wrapped in old newspaper, or an old box of smarties. We didn't care. It was all so exciting. Mammy looked on in horror.

"Mammy, don't be giving them that rubbish," she exclaimed.

"It won't do them any harm. You're too fussy sometimes, Pat."

One day, we heard a strange sound coming from her basket. She dug down deep and out of the brown reed came a black and white furry ball. It was a puppy.

"Mammy, ye didn't pick up a stray dog. Ah, now Mammy, this is too much." But Mammy's protests fell on deaf ears.

"Can we keep him, please?" My brothers and I piped up.

Grandmammy lifted her glass and made a toast to the 'new puppy'. He was christened 'Whiskey' when she lifted her glass. Or that's what we assumed his name was!

"Whiskey, his name is Whiskey," we exclaimed. Mammy just rolled her eyes to the heavens.

Grandmammy would always ask that I should walk her down to the bus stop.

"Let the child spread her wings, for God's sake, Pat," she slurred.

I waited at the bus stop until her bus would come and wave her off into the distance.

Normally, she was not a cuddly type but this time, she took me in her arms. I sniffed her strange smell.

"Child, beware of wolves in sheep's clothing," she said, clear as can be.

I kissed her dry skin. I loved her.

She had a stroke a few weeks later and died.

"Children don't go to funerals," Mammy said.

Grandmammy disappeared out of our lives as easily as she had come into it. My brothers and I were used to people leaving. I cried uncontrollably in my bedroom but Whiskey was in my life now. Whiskey was my own border collie and we became inseparable. He would wait for me outside school and would run alongside me on the bike. He was my reason to disappear from Mammy's prying eyes.

"Mammy, I'm just going for a walk in 'Bushy Park' with Whiskey," I'd say. Whiskey ran like the wind and I followed him, my long hair flowing in the wind. I screamed into the air and whoopied through the whole park.

I would call out "I'm going to catch you, Whiskey," or "Where are the nuns?" He went berserk when I said the word 'nuns'. "Hunt them down and kill them!" I loved our time together, but I went home muddy and dishevelled.

"Where have you been with that dog? Look at the state of you," Mammy cried.

Whiskey growled.

"Mammy, I had to run after Whiskey in case he ran in front of a car. I had to go through the field to catch him," I exclaimed.

Whiskey would look at me and we would disappear to do my homework. I would get out my finger puppets and Whiskey would try and rip them off my fingers. He would bark with frustration as I removed them and put them in my secret box under my bed. He was my friend and constant companion.

CHAPTER 11

TWELVE
MY FIRST BRA

Thankfully, most nuns were only able to teach at primary level. At secondary school, although they were still very much present, their power was reduced and became manageable. The teachers were obliged to say a morning prayer before starting class but apart from our religious teachers, there was not really a problem. We even had male teachers. I was terrified when Mr McInerney came in and introduced himself as the new biology teacher. His red hair and face made him look permanently embarrassed. In time, when he explained some of the facts of life to us, it became apparent why he was constantly red.

I was so pleased not to have to endure the nuns that I skipped into school. I had had seven full years of cruelty. Now and again, I would meet a nun in the corridor.

"And how is the harlot getting on?" she'd ask.

"Grand. The harlot is doing great," I would reply. I knew not to go too far with my comments. The nuns were always hovering around the next corner ready to take a dig at me.

One day, Mother Patrick came into the class. We were having a history lesson with Mr Caffrey. She asked if she could interrupt the lesson for a minute and proceeded to call out names from a list she held in her wrinkled hands.

These girls were to come to the office.

Of course, my name was on the list. But I was relieved when other names were called and about five of us were frog-marched down to the office.

"It has come to our attention that your pinafores are too tight on top," we were told. "This is leading the male teachers to become distracted. You will go home immediately and ask your mothers to remove the top part of the pinafore and come back to school with a very loose shirt tucked into your skirt."

I went straight home. Mammy flew into a panic.

"I'm not the only one," I assured her.

I went to Mrs McNamara next door and she expertly unpicked the top of the pinafore, used the cloth to make a waistband and I had a skirt in no time at all. Mrs McNamara was a wizard on the sewing machine. Mammy tucked my shirt loosely into my skirt.

"Now, Niamh, will you put on an extra vest to flatten that chest a bit more?"

"No," I said. "This is ridiculous, Mammy. I need to get a bra. Some of the other girls in my class have them."

"Do they now?"

"Indeed they do, Mammy."

And Mammy reluctantly relented.

While I had her in a conciliatory mood, I begged her to take me to town that weekend and she agreed.

I went back to school with my new look. Each girl had been given two hours to go home. My skirt had a lovely band around the waist and was neat and tidy. But some of the other girls had had to cut and sew a temporary solution themselves. One girl had made a kind of belt out of elastic bands, linked together to hold up her rapidly fraying waistband. Her mother worked and so was not at home. The nuns gave her a hard time about her mother working and the poor girl tried to keep the skirt up the whole afternoon. Luckily, I had some safety pins and some other girls had hat pins and so we gathered round to help her attach the skirt to her shirt so that it didn't fall off.

I formed a sort of bond with these girls. Later, the nuns changed the rule and pinafores were only worn the first year in secondary school. After that, skirts had to be worn. Our womanly forms had to be hidden from the outside world. We were a walking temptation. I had been labelled a whore for so long that it didn't touch me but when some of the other girls were given the label too, it gave me a sense of belonging. It was always the girls with the bigger breasts who were called whores.

These girls took things lightly and it made me feel good to be around such rebellious beings. They would laugh into the faces of the nuns.

"We're all brazen hussies. So let's behave like that," Pauline said.

Pauline's father owned the local pub and her diet consisted mainly of crisps and lemonade. Her mother and father were always busy working in the pub.

"That poor child has been dragged up. Did you see the state of her?" I heard Mammy say.

Pauline tugged at a slightly greasy lock of her dark hair and grinned mischievously.

She brought card boxes filled with Tayto crisps to school and would hide them behind the bicycle shed. The 'hussy' gang would inevitably meet up there and scoff the lot.

I didn't know how to behave like a hussy, and they didn't either, so we just made jokes and laughed when the nuns approached. I always tried to stick close to my big-chested friends. I felt safer with them. Now and again, a nun would catch me on my own.

"We're watching the likes of you and your whores. You'll never come to anything,' she'd say.

"You're rotten through and through. You're the bad apple in the cart. You will contaminate everything that you touch."

I threw up the crisps on the way home. Whiskey looked at me sadly from under the old willow tree. The branches seemed to reach out to me and I bashed them back out of the way angrily. Whiskey growled at the invisible enemy.

"Whiskey, it's weigh-in night. Mammy can't know." It was Friday and Mammy had the pink weighing scales in the bathroom ready and waiting. The pink furry covering had been bought to make it look nice.

I had nightmares in which I was rotting away in a big cardboard box and the nuns were digging me out with their nails.

I did my best to remember what Ronka had said to me: "You are more than words, Niamh . . ." But the daily abuse had done its damage.

I didn't think about what had happened when I was nine. Not ever. That experience had been locked away in some deep recess of my mind. It had been locked into a wardrobe in my memory and the key had been thrown away. It was easier that way.

My trip to purchase my first bra was unforgettable. I was going on thirteen. Mammy and I dressed up in our best clothes and took the bus into town. The jolting of the old bus made me feel sick and apprehensive. The suspension had seen better days.

"Jesus, it's like sitting in the rodeo on this bloody bus," exclaimed Mammy.

"We can always turn back," I said. "We can go another day."

"No," my mother replied. "We're almost there and looking at you now, it is very clear that you need an uplift."

I looked around in the bus, hoping that nobody had heard. An 'uplift'. It sounded like a place where you went and the lift took you up to other places. I remember grinning to myself and thinking, where would my breasts go? How far could they be lifted up?

The very idea of the trip was even more frightening now. Why had I even suggested such a thing? I was going to pay the price. At the same time, it was quite exciting. I'd known for a while that it was hard to have pleasure without the pain. I didn't often get the opportunity to go into town with Mammy. We smiled at each other and I took her hand. These moments were very precious to me and I placed my head on her shoulder. I knew that pleased her and I felt warm and safe inside. An old woman sat down opposite us.

"A fine girl you have there," she said to my mother. "What a head of hair on her!"

My mother looked proudly at me.

"We'll get some chamomile tea while we are in town," she whispered. "It's great for keeping your hair blonde. I'll put the tea in the last rinse."

I used to have to surrender to a strict routine that involved my hair being washed, rinsed, washed and rinsed again. The ritual took at least an hour and as I got older, I started to protest.

"Your hair is your crowning glory," she would reply. "You have to suffer a little to be beautiful."

What kind of suffering would take place at my uplifting, I wondered? I had visions of my poor young breasts being squashed into oblivion. I had seen my mother's bras. They were pretty intricate contraptions. Mammy had her theories about a good bra.

"A good strong strap, you'll need, Niamh, and strong seams underneath for support," she advised.
Mammy knew about these things.

When Mammy got an idea in her head, it had to be accomplished. She knew where she was going and I fell in with her military step. We had to walk a while through the narrow back streets of Dublin before we found the "special shop".

"If you are going to be fitted for your first bra, this is the best shop in town," she said. "They have been doing this for years,"

It sounded like a military operation. I saw the determined look on my mother's face. There was no turning back.

We walked into a small narrow shop that was sandwiched between two grocery stores and overflowed with boxes and all kinds of cotton vests, and underpants of every size and variety. Elderly women were hovering in the narrow corridor, feeling and stretching white cotton garments with concentrated looks on their faces.

"Marie, I want a nice wide gusset," my mother said. "Have you got these in my size?"

Marie was the smallest lady I had ever seen in my life. Suddenly she appeared beside us. It was as if she had sprung from out of one of the cardboard boxes. Her little legs seemed to run ahead of her and her large head would follow, twitching involuntarily. To a thirteen-year-old, she was terrifying. She trotted towards us and I stepped back to hide behind my mother. But because I was taller I could still see this strange little person over my mother's head.

"Ah there you are Pat!" she said. "And is this your baby?"

My mother always explained to people that she had three children and that I was the baby. Even if you were an adult, Irish mothers would refer to you as 'the baby'.

"She is, she is," my mother replied, pushing me forward. I knew she knew Mammy well. Only her friends called her 'Pat'.

Marie smiled at me and it was such a wonderful, warm smile that it melted my heart.

"Is this your first time, my dear?" she asked.

"Yes," I stammered as Marie looked me up and down very slowly and rubbed her chin in thought.

"Pat, I have some great new Berlei bras in for teenagers," she said. "They have gingham prints. I'll go and get them. In the meantime, bring her into the back of the shop so we can measure her."

A few older women started chatting to my mother.

"Ah, is it her first time?" they all asked. "Isn't she a grand girl!"

"My Maura got her first one here and has never looked back."

"I've been coming here 30 years, you know. Marie knows everything about bosoms. Yes, everything, inside and out."

I was hoping I would not have to undress in front of Marie. But her knowledge of 'them' was legendary. I was led into a little cubicle. It was so small that only one person could fit into it. Phew, I thought, Mammy won't be able to come in. Instead Marie appeared in front of me. She was so small that it seemed she could fit anywhere. She had a little wooden box to stand on. Around her shoulders, she had a white measuring tape.

"Now, sweetheart, show us what you've got," she said. "I have a feeling that you are a 34A."

I had taken off my T-shirt and stood in my two vests. She placed the tape around my back and measured me.

"Pat, she's only an A!" she called out. "Hold on a minute, take off the vests so that we can really see what's going on there."

She was having an ongoing discussion with my mother who was parked outside the cubicle.

"No, Patricia, she's a B. The poor child was suffocating in those tight vests."

She surveyed my bare breasts. I looked down at them for the first time in years. They were perky and pretty and my nipples were pink and seemed to stick out.

"She'll have no trouble feeding the babies when the time comes Patricia. They are grand, grand," declared Marie.

"Grand, grand," came my mother's reply.

I had not the foggiest idea what they were talking about. How could I feed babies? I thought that they were talking a secret code. For me, I thought of the freedom of not wearing tight vests anymore and how heavenly that would be.

My mother, it seemed, had decided to acknowledge that I had breasts at long last. Four years of fighting their growth had come to an end. Her logic never ceased to amaze me. She had decided that it was time I had breasts and they were allowed to be seen now.

"Marie, make sure she knows how to place them properly in the bra," Mammy said and I heard a quiver in her voice.

A cup of tea was given to Mammy by a young assistant whose sole duty, as far as I could see, was to hand out cups of steaming tea to tired customers.

Marie then pulled aside the cubicle curtain with a flourish and Mammy surveyed my new Berlei bra. It was sky-blue gingham and felt very comfortable indeed.

"Niamh, now don't slouch, shoulders back," said my mother. "You're not a hangman's daughter." This was Mammy's way of saying that I had to lift up my head high. I had nothing to be ashamed of.

I stuck my chest out and took a deep breath. Marie and my mother drank in the sight of me in my bra and undies.

"Sure Patricia, she'll be a heartbreaker one of these days," Marie said. "What a figure on her and her so young."

Mammy said nothing. Tears formed in her bright blue eyes. I was confused. The happy moment was over. I was going to break people's hearts and that was not a good thing. I wanted to go home. But Marie and my mother became quite animated and started talking about old times. I think they must have known each other from school.

My mother never spoke about her childhood. I strained to listen out for snippets of information but then they lowered their voices further so that all I heard was muffled whispering.

A big-breasted woman who was waiting on the cubicle approached.

"Marie, I think the double F is going to be too small," she said.

"Not at all, Aine, it's all in the back with you. Your chest is not that big," replied Marie.

I didn't quite know what that meant but I remember looking at Aine's back and yes, it was broad. I had had to flatten myself against the small cubicle so that she could get in alongside me.

"Niamh, will ye let Aine in there and you get dressed? Would you like the pink gingham too? You might as well keep the blue one on. Remember, don't slouch, or you will get a hump on your back."

Mammy was going to buy me a second bra! I stuck out my chest and straightened my back. We had all seen *the Hunchback of Notre Dame* on the television. My mother had told my brothers and I that he had got that hump from bending over too much. We were famous for our correct postures after that.

"Would you look at the O'Broin family?" they'd say. "Fine, straight and handsome."

I was so surprised by my mother's new acceptance of my bosom that I couldn't bring myself to reply. She took that for an affirmative and by the time I was fully dressed, my other bra had been wrapped in tissue and put in a lovely pink bag. I felt strangely uplifted and thought I knew now what my mother had meant.

I looked down at my perky shape and caught my reflection in one of the long mirrors in the shop. My breasts had been hidden for such a long time. Now, they could come out and be part of my new world. I felt slightly distanced from them and yet I knew that they were part of me. I was just glad that they had the freedom that they deserved. After all, four years of imprisonment was a long time. I sang a little ode to my breasts.

"At last the time has come to take you out into the big wide world

Stay uplifted and free and hopefully become a part of me."

My mother decided that the occasion should be marked by a cup of tea and a sticky bun at Bewley's in Grafton Street. Bewley's is one of the most famous tea houses in Dublin. I took my mother's hand and I knew she loved me. I felt such fondness and empathy for her and I looked into her lovely face with its worried frown. She looked back at me and I saw her difficulty with accepting the passing of time. I knew she was doing her best so I would do my best for her. This seminal day signified a new start for us both.

I was allowed two sticky buns and a chocolate éclair. It must have been a very special occasion indeed. I looked down at my perky shape and decided that breasts weren't that bad after all.

"Now, Niamh," my mother said, "they will be looking more often at you so be careful of strangers and never get into strange cars."

I hadn't the heart to tell my mother that the dangers I faced were much closer to home. A cold sweat engulfed me and fear gripped my stomach. I prayed that I would not throw up. The sticky buns with their almond centres had been delicious and I had generously buttered them too. But once we were back in the bus I began to worry that I would now be attractive to dangerous men and that one would leap out of the shadows and take me away.

"The devil moves in mysterious ways," Mother Joseph had said to me. "He will kiss you and caress you and you will give in to his wicked ways. His serpent tongue will find you and lick your body into temptation." She had wiped her sweaty forehead on her black bat-like sleeve.

Every man that happened to glance my way on the bus terrified me. I was so panic-stricken by the time we got home that I ran into the house and hid in the closet under the stairs. We called it the 'cloakroom' because all our coats and jackets were kept there. I stayed there until I was called for dinner. My mother assumed I was just overwhelmed by my new purchases.

"Mammy, can I put my vests on tomorrow?" I asked.

"Jesus, Mary and Joseph, you will not," she exclaimed. "After all we have been through. You'll put on your bra and be done with it."

I was afraid the nuns would notice my new shape and tucked my school shirt very loosely into my waistband. I had to wear a fine white vest over the bra to mask the blue checks that showed through the white shirt and that comforted me a little.

I made sure that I hunched over when I passed the nuns in the corridor and nothing was said that day.

I always tried to make myself as inconspicuous as possible but my long blond hair and height made it difficult sometimes. I developed a couple of tricks that would make me almost invisible. I walked at the very edge of the corridor, near the walls. I would take long strides and move stealthily until I got to my class. Or, sometimes I would try to find a group and walk with them so that I could get away more easily if approached. Although it was exhausting trying to avoid the nuns all the time, I became a master of planning and strategy.

Inevitably though, one of them would catch me off guard.

"You are looking very angelic today. You don't deceive us. We know the whore that you are," they'd whisper in my ear.

"The devil knows what you are thinking and so do we."

"We are all-seeing and all-knowing."

CHAPTER 12

SIXTEEN
TRAGEDY

I sat on a pier wall in Dun Laoghaire, in Dublin, praying that the waves would take me away. I sat there for hours waiting, but they never did. I cried out to my creator and cursed him for making me this way. The waves bashed against the pier wall. I was miserable and felt alone. My mother and I were in constant battle at home.

"Niamh, don't eat that now. You were doing so well. You won't fit into those lovely Wrangler jeans."

"Please can I go to town with some of the girls?"

"It's too dangerous. Somebody might kidnap you and you will never be seen again. I read somewhere…"

My mother didn't go out much but read in the local papers about the dreadful happenings that took place. She knew that "the most rapes are committed in the middle of the day" and that "slender women are the most successful".

She insisted on washing my hair still and my bath time was also overseen by her. The bathroom would have to be left unlocked so that my mother could peek in to inspect my developing body.

"What's that on your back, is that a pimple?" Or "Watch the weight now, just a little bit more off your legs."

It was a constant onslaught of intense control. I began to resent Mammy more and more.

My brothers were getting on with their lives. They were coming and going meeting friends and playing their rugby matches. I was stuck in some sort of fish bowl. I had dreams of swimming in an orange bikini and a big eye inspecting me through a gigantic magnifying glass. The eye looked suspiciously like Mammy's. I had nowhere to run.

One afternoon, my mother had been to town and I'd searched the whole house for her secret chocolate stash. Whiskey sniffed around her bedroom and I found a huge box of Cadbury's chocolates under her bed.

"Well done, Whiskey." I petted the beautiful white star on his forehead. I removed the first layer of chocolates and ate the second. I then replaced the empty tray and put the first layer back. Unfortunately, this box of chocolates was meant as a birthday present for Mammy's friend. She rang Mammy later to tell her that the chocolates had been tampered with. Terrified of my mother's wrath, I'd gone to the pier to talk to Daddy, miles and miles away at sea. I'd talk to the waves before going home to face the music. To make matters worse, I felt I couldn't face another day at school. The constant pressure was getting to me. My intermediate certificate was coming up and Daddy had sent me a letter.

"I know you will do well, my golden princess," he had written. "We need never worry about you."

My parents had given more freedom to my brothers and they went their own way. Mammy could not control two teenage boys on her own and their rugby antics and drinking was pretty much accepted. All Mammy's focus was on me. She'd make her imperfect daughter perfect. It was her sole mission in life. Daddy thought that I already was perfect. I was his golden princess. I felt alone and trapped. No one gave me the chance to be myself.

The sea had always attracted me. Her strength and wildness beckoned me to her. I screamed and roared as the waves plunged against the pier wall. Splashes of sea spray sprinkled on my face. What if I just jumped in and joined the waves? I longed to ride with them back to wherever they came from. I longed to disappear into the ocean, never to be seen again. But then I imagined my mother waiting for me at home. She'd be furious about the chocolates. She would look at my figure accusingly and that would be punishment enough. I couldn't hurt my father either. I was his one and only golden princess. As I resignedly got the bus back to Dublin, I looked back and saw a seagull sweeping down into the sea and wished that that could be me. I boarded the bus with a heavy heart. Whiskey followed me with his fluffy tail between his legs.

"Let's go home and face the music, boy," I said softly. Whiskey placed his wet nose on my lap in the crowded bus.

Mammy was at the door.

"You can't be trusted. Imagine doing that! You're a sneak and a thief!" she screamed. Her face was flushed with anger and she glared at me with fire in her eyes. Whiskey growled at her. She backed off.

I didn't care anymore. I went upstairs and vomited the life out of me. The chocolate brown flecks being flushed down the toilet reminded me of the swirling sea beneath the pier. I leaned against the bowl and cried. I cried for all the times I had been called whore and harlot, and I cried for being called a sneak and a thief.

I opened up my geography book and traced the map of Ireland onto my exercise book. I realised that I was on an island and had no way to get off it. I got out my blue biro pen.

"Please get me out of here," I wrote on the map. "I'm drowning."

It was May and Daddy was coming home for three whole months until August. I couldn't wait. I had been practicing in the kitchen like mad on my guitar. My teacher had instructed all his students to give a recital to their family and friends to show their progress. Daddy would be home for this recital. I would have to do him proud. Whiskey sat at my feet whilst I sang and sang for hours to get it right.

"Niamh, it's a great song. You are my star pupil," Carl Alfred said to me. He was my guitar teacher, originally from the Caribbean. Daddy had enrolled me in his classes. His dark hands were placed over mine. I lived for my weekly lessons.

"Padraicin, get up those stairs and get ready. We are all going to see Niamh Chinn Oir perform," Daddy boomed at Mammy. There was no escape from it. Mammy had to come too. She preferred to stay at home. I saw all the family and friends sitting in the large old-fashioned room, surrounded by colourful paintings of Carl's tropical past. A lot of the students performed before me and I got more and more nervous, waiting for my turn. I fixed my pink top and pulled down my black velvet skirt. I was a bit wobbly on my new black suede boots. They were quite high and I hoped that I would not fall.

"Now, we have Niamh. She has come such a long way in such a short time. Just listen to her and you will know what I mean. A big round of applause for Niamh," Carl announced in his lilting Caribbean accent.

I came out and started my special song for Daddy.

"I would like to dedicate this song to my Daddy and Mammy. It's called 'Vincent'." I bowed my head to the guitar and began to sing.

I finished my song. I stood up and gave a gracious bow. The one Mammy had taught me in the kitchen, night after night.

There was a silence in the air. I panicked inside and then suddenly the whole room burst into applause. It was so loud and it was all for me. I couldn't believe it. I bowed again and again. It wouldn't stop. I saw Daddy and Mammy in the audience, clapping and clapping. They looked so happy. They were together.

After the performances, Carl had arranged a tropical buffet with tangy fruit salads and food I had never tasted before. Everybody came up to me to congratulate me on my performance. Daddy waited until he had a quiet moment with me and then he took me in his arms and gave me one of his bear hugs. I looked into his tear-filled eyes and saw a reflection of my own sadness. It was a mirror. I was startled at this revelation.

"Niamh Chinn Oir, never stop singing. You have the gift," he said to me.

Mammy kissed me and congratulated me on my performance. My parents were together for something important in my life. My brothers weren't there but that didn't matter to me. I knew that Daddy understood me.

Daddy's presence was felt during the next months. He was going to take us out individually for a day. My brothers had already had their 'special' time with Daddy.

Croquet competitions had been organized in the back garden for the local children. Noisy boys invaded the house yet again. Daddy made a volleyball net and supervised gangly boys trying to behave like men. Parents were invited in. The whole community loved it when Daddy came home.

Mammy made her famous 'Frankenstein' sponges. They were called that because they were square and had so much cream filling in them. The weather was fabulous and we all ran around in our shorts and t-shirts. Daddy's tanned legs stood out from the crowd. The other daddies had white skinny legs. Daddy was the first man to wear Bermuda shorts in the street. He also wore open sandals with no socks. I loved to look at his brown toes peeping out of his leather sandals. I saw the other mammies looking at him. Daddy was very handsome indeed.

"Niamh, it's your turn today. I have to go to the American Embassy for my visa. Let's make a day of it." Whiskey stayed at home. He looked at us forlornly as we walked down the street, arm in arm. Mammy waved us off. A part of me wanted her to come too.

Daddy and I sat in Herbert Park in Ballsbridge in Dublin. The sun shone through the trees and we licked our ice-creams. I held his hand very tightly. Daddy didn't seem to mind. His strong rough hands were so comforting. I wanted to savour every minute with him.

"Daddy, I'll never sing that song again. That was

especially for you." And I meant it. I never did, as it turned out.

We did some shopping and Daddy bought me a pair of red and yellow platform shoes.

"The nuns would go mad if you went to school in them," he grinned broadly.

"Don't worry Daddy, I'll only wear them on special occasions," I laughed back.

We got home later in the evening. I couldn't sleep thinking of the wonderful day that we had had together.

Daddy came in to say goodnight.

"Daddy, will you tuck me in?" I asked.

"Niamh, you're a bit old for that now, aren't you?" he smiled but did it anyway. He wrapped me up in my duvet and exaggeratedly tucked me in.

Dad had just got his captain's papers and was so proud. He was waiting for his own ship.

"I'll be captain soon and we can afford a lot more things, Padraicín," he had said. This would be his last run as first mate.

I remember him studying very early in the morning at the kitchen table. I would come down and we would breakfast together. We would have 'bubble and squeak', which was fried potatoes and onions and leftover vegetables made into little balls. We would roll them together and place them in the raging oil, jumping back to avoid the splashes.

"Your mother will go mad at the mess we have made," he said, winking at me.

These were our special moments, our special times.

The three months went very fast indeed. Soon, it was time for Daddy to go again. He left on a rainy day in August.

I looked outside at the windy weather. It was October and I hoped my umbrella would stay up. I was getting ready for my guitar class and had packed my guitar into its case. Mammy was upstairs and my brothers were in the dining room looking at television.

The doorbell rang. I answered it. Two men were standing at the door. One was Father Lee, the local parish priest. The other was dressed in a beautifully tailored suit and fawn trench coat. He had a briefcase in his hand.

"Is your mother home?" Father Lee asked.

"Father, I'll get her for you," I said, shouting up the stairs to my mother.

Mammy was not pleased. We assumed they were from the church, asking for money. Many a time we had not answered the door for them. We would sometimes hide and wait until the collectors would leave. My mother could be very funny at times. She would duck unexpectedly under the big sitting-room window until all was clear. We would all break out into hysterical giggles afterwards. But this was different. I could feel it in my bones.

Father Lee looked at my mother.

"Mrs O'Broin," he said, "when was the last time you heard from your husband?"

Silence ensued. My mother took a deep breath and invited them in. She led them into the living room and I followed suit. I had an overwhelming feeling that I had to be there.

The man in the business suit introduced himself as a representative of Athel Line ships. This was the company Daddy worked for. The man looked like a cold fish. His eyes were light blue and he moved his mouth like a cod. He said words but I could not understand them. I remember screaming. My brothers ran in to the room.

"I am very sorry to inform you that your husband has been killed at sea," the man said. "We do not have a lot of details at the moment but it seems that there was a storm in the South China Seas. Your husband acted above and beyond the call of duty and helped the crew batten down some leaking hatches. A freak wave engulfed him and threw him from the foc'sle onto the lower deck. What we can gather is that he died of head injuries a few hours later. He has already been buried at sea. That was his request. We have his details from administration here, on a form he had filled in when he first joined us. We await further instructions. They will fax me back at the hotel. I am very sorry for your loss."

I looked around our sitting room and saw the white cupboard that Dad had so lovingly made. He had copied it from a furniture magazine and the salon table was in matching white and had little wheels. My mother had been delighted with the end result. We used to have afternoon tea and roll the table from place to place just for the sake of it.

I saw my father's strong bronzed face smiling and him putting his arms around his small wife. I caught him winking at me and I smiled back at him. His twinkling blue eyes were shining against his tanned frame. I couldn't bear to think of his head being smashed against the ship's metal. Daddy, don't go away, I pleaded. I closed my eyes and tried to imprint his image in my mind. My whole world had been taken away from me.

My mother remained calm and Turlough took me, still screaming, in his arms. She calmly told Eoghan to ring her friend Ena. We sat in the living room shell-shocked. Eoghan could not cry and the acid of his unshed tears made his eyes swell up. I held his hand tightly. Whiskey placed his head on my lap. His white star looked dark in the silence. The events afterwards remain a blur.

When they brought the news of Daddy's death, I thought it was my fault. I had begged the sea to take me but she had taken my father instead. He had been my one salvation in all the insanity around me. We had played guitar and sung together. We had read and sat together. He had listened to me. I had hungrily sucked in every morsel of attention he gave me. Daddy had taken me away from a controlling situation. He had even been known to speak up to my mother and correct her. I would never lay eyes on him again. He had not just been my father. He had been my friend.

My father hated St Pious, the local church. He said he would not even shelter from the rain in it. They had put so much money into this church, he said, but left the school in its pre-fabricated condition. He had protested vehemently and led a petition. But it fell on deaf ears. That is why we hardly ever attended the church. It was a matter of principle. My father was a man of great principle.

Mammy was adamant.

"The funeral service will not be held in that monstrosity," she said.

We all agreed. I remember walking many a time with Whiskey and Daddy past the church and he would grit his teeth and walk faster.

Mammy was a tower of strength and organised whatever had to be done. Her friends rallied around and many warm meals were put outside the door so that my mother didn't have to cook.

I tried not to think of his body somewhere else far away from us. I couldn't bear to think of him being all on his own out there somewhere. I lay awake at night hoping that this was all a dream. But my dreams only clarified the situation. Daddy was dead. He came to me, all bloodied and pale, even there, in my dreams.

The local Holy Ghost Fathers offered a private ceremony just for the four of us in their private chapel. We had no body and no coffin. I thought that Daddy would walk in on us and laugh at the situation. I kept on looking out for him. It didn't seem real.

We had the most beautiful service in the small chapel in the grounds of the Holy Ghost Fathers and we felt calmness in us. I remember feeling that this was the end of our lives as we knew it. It was not only the death of our father that we were grieving.

I watched my two brothers standing tall and proud. Only their heads hung in deference, one at each side of my mother. Her small frame was dwarfed by their lean bodies. I was looking in on the situation. I felt I was watching them with my father at my side. I had no song in me. I felt nothing except guilt. I looked down at my red and yellow shoes.

"Jesus, Niamh, you're not wearing them, not today," Mammy shouted.

"I am, I bloody well am. Don't stop me," I screamed. She turned away with her hands in the air.

"Daddy, forgive me. It should have been me."

Unfortunately, the local parish priest was in a bit of a situation. The representatives of Daddy's company were coming over from Britain for a big church service. Father Lee told Mammy that he was instructed by the British representatives to arrange an appropriate funeral mass. This meant that my mother and the rest of the family would have to come to the occasion. My mother protested vehemently but eventually sat us down and said to us.

"We have already had our special mass for Dad in our little chapel. Dad won't mind if we are guests at the other big sham of a do put on for the British. I know he hated that bloody church but we will not let him down now. We will all be on our best behaviour and we will even have them to the house for tea after the ceremony. We will make him proud."

We all agreed and it was a welcome distraction for us to get the house ready for the 'big shots' coming over from England.

I helped put out our best china and Mammy's friends made a beautiful buffet of cold meats, salads and wonderful cakes and puddings. The table was stylishly arranged with Waterford crystal glasses, which had been dusted and shone to perfection. All Mammy's best bone china was elegantly on display. Mammy had an eye for such things. I knew that she wanted the house looking perfect. These representatives were to walk into the home of a respected seaman. My mother was determined that Dad's memory would not be sullied. This helped her distract herself from thinking about the future.

We all went to the big church that my father hated. It was packed full. I saw the decadent chandeliers and fabulous stained glass windows. I had taken my first Holy Communion and been confirmed here. But this time, it was different. The British representatives were seated in the front rows and we took a back seat. We were invited to sit at the front but my mother refused. Even my school class came along. We endured it willingly, for Mammy's sake.

The people of the congregation waited at the door in a line to give us their condolences. But my mother had another plan. Her girlfriend had a car waiting for us at the back of the church. We slipped out and made a run for it. The congregation did not realise that we were gone. My mother had her sweet revenge. The neighbours that she loathed lined up in docile lines but the star never turned up and they left disappointed and annoyed. They had heard that our family would receive a large sum of money from the 'bigwigs'. The rumour had to be confirmed and discussed, but nobody was there to confirm or deny it.

I looked back as we were being whisked away in the car. Some of my school friends had come out of the church. I waved but they did not see me. A part of me wanted to stay and share in the tragedy. I imagined all the whisperings and shaking of heads.

The stark Roman pillars my father despised stood white and tall. A sea of black emerged suddenly from the entrance. The nuns shuffled between the columns, searching in vain. I ducked down further into the back seat. I saw one of my more timid classmates, Anne, surrounded by them. Pauline had managed to escape from the black invasion, but Anne looked bewildered and her thin frame seemed even smaller in the circle of darkness. She was pushed out of the way.

"Well, the whore of Babylon has no one to look out for her now. Where is she?"

I knew that Anne would tell me later what had actually been said.

The British officials arrived at our house, breathless and slightly put out. My mother answered the door and welcomed them inside. She put on her best 'telephone' voice as we used to call it.

"Welcome to our home. There is tea and light refreshments. The buffet is in the dining room."

She laughed about it for years afterwards.

"We were whipped away like royalty," she laughed, "I wish I could've seen their faces when they were looking for us!"

We should have stayed and faced our enemies. My father would never have approved of us running away from confrontation. I felt slightly ashamed when one middle-aged British official approached me.

"How are you holding up, me love?" he asked. I saw genuine compassion in his brown eyes. He was the first person to ask and I stammered that I was doing okay. He patted my hand and moved back into the crowd standing on the other side of the dining room.

I realised then that it was real. My daddy wasn't coming back. My brothers were mingling, going from one group to another. Turlough, tall and extroverted, made a comment and everybody burst out laughing. He always was the charmer. Eoghan, stockier and quiet, always in his brother's shadow, did his best to socialise. He glanced over at me and I blew him a kiss. His bloodshot eyes crinkled into a hesitant smile. I knew that I would have to be there for him. The future was suddenly very uncertain. I shuddered and left the scene. I sneaked a cream cake upstairs and ate it voraciously, standing up, leaning against the bedroom door. The cream mingled on my lips with the salty water of my tears. Whiskey stayed in the shadows.

Mammy coped admirably that day and I loved her for it. She flitted from one person to the next like a little butterfly, moving so fast it became almost a dance. She was trying to please everyone, not having eaten all day. Some glasses had accidentally been put on the trolley. My mother placed coasters under them and I saw her touching the white glossy wood. Her quivering lip was the only thing that gave her away. She straightened up and started clearing away some plates and tea cups. I imagined Daddy standing there, sliding his arm around the waist of his grieving widow.

"I am so proud of you all," Mammy told us after everybody had left. "Your dad would have been so proud of you." But her lip trembled.

The lawyers sat down with my mother and told her that the accident had been an act of God, which meant that we were not entitled to any compensation for the freak wave that took his life.

"I'll rear you for the next few years and then my task is done," my mother said to us. "And then I'll join Paddy."

I was terrified that she would die and leave us. For weeks afterwards we received post from Daddy, letters he had sent before he died, letters from different ports. It made the situation more unreal. I waited for the postman anxiously.

My brothers and I were scarred terribly by the tragedy. Turlough felt that he had to be the man of the house. He was nineteen and had just started his first job in marine insurance. This was a lot of responsibility on such a young man's shoulders and it took its toll.

Eoghan said nothing and left his job in car insurance.

"We'll give him a while to recover before he looks for a new job", Mammy said. In the meantime, Eoghan sat in a darkened living room looking at a blank screen on the television. I couldn't help him. I continued to believe that I was responsible for my father's death. I cried out in the night and asked for forgiveness for being such a worthless human being.

"Forgive me Daddy. The sea took you instead of me.

Take me with you and we'll be together forever and ever."

I knew that I had to be strong and take care of Mammy. I never saw her cry but I did see a broken woman. She had loved my father deeply and although he had spent more than half of their married life at sea, she could not do without him. Her life had centred on him coming home and then leaving again. There was no in between.

Indeed the whole family had lived for him coming home. We were lost souls without him. He was the tall tree that grounded us in our mossy soil. Our roots were weak when we were without him.

The photos of the burial service at sea were sent to my mother. She was sitting having a cup of tea when the postman came. My mother wouldn't let me see them. But I found them later and took a peek. I saw the Union Jack displayed over the body bag and his body being thrown to the furious sea. Uniformed men surrounded the bag, saluting a final farewell.

He is buried in the South China Seas, faraway from us all in some obscure ocean. I touched the photos, trying to make sense of things. I thought of his beautiful strong body being fed to the fishes. I cried out for him in the night and wanted to join him. I felt betrayed and alone. I had visions of him being eaten by sharks. I could not bear to think of him on the sea bottom, his blue eyes torn apart by the savage beasts of the sea.

"Niamh, the bag was made of very strong canvas and no fish could penetrate it," Turlough told me. "Dad's body will eventually disintegrate and become part of the sea floor."

He said it matter of factly, trying to convince me that it would be okay. He has my father's blue eyes and he wiped away a tear as he spoke. I was a little consoled. But I just imagined pieces of Daddy scattered over a coral reef. He loved the coral reefs of Australia. I had all kinds of nightmares about how he died and it was there in my dreams that I tried to make sense of his death. I was angry with him for helping the young cadets. It was so typical of him, always ready to give a helping hand. He gave his life for some stupid leaking hatches. I had whole conversations with him about why he should not have done it. The silence of the night seemed to emphasise my own betrayal.

I started cutting myself in my groin area, where the marks would not be seen. I had nowhere to go with my intense, excruciating pain. I found a small knife in Dad's toolbox and made long, slashing cuts into my pale skin. These scars would be a testament to my pain. I opened and re-opened my wounds time and time again. The blood dripped down my legs. It was familiar yet disgusting. My head was a whirlpool of desperation. My poor mother had enough to deal with. Eoghan was becoming increasingly introverted. But Daddy had always said: "Keep problems within the family. That is the honour of the family." So we did. Mammy and I helped Eoghan as much as we could. What else could I do?

Turlough had decided to move to America to pursue a deep-sea diving career. Now it was up to me to hold it together now, for the family.

"Whiskey, love me for who I am," I cried, holding him tightly and gratefully. He licked my salty tears and I knew he felt my pain.

I was going into my final year, preparing for my Leaving Certificate.

"Do your dad proud," Mammy said. "Study and do the best you can."

There was no money for me to be sent to university. My father and I had plotted and planned for my Trinity college education. I left that dream by the wayside. I was on automatic pilot and the nuns didn't bother with me anymore. Their anger was now directed at some other poor young soul. I almost envied their new punch bag. She had flaxen curls and an angelic face. I hated her too. I saw too much of me in her and avoided her hunched figure walking down the corridor. I simply had no feeling any more.

Fight back you stupid bitch, I thought. Fight back, I said to her, silently.

I tried every trick in the book to get the teachers to punish me for something, anything. Pain and humiliation reminded me that I was alive. It was an escape from the agonising reality of a home life spent with a mother and brother who were slipping slowly into madness and despair.

My behaviour was appalling but they decided to ignore it. They felt sorry for my loss. I saw pity in their eyes. I hated them even more. My last year in school was one of rage. I hated everybody and anyone. I wanted to be left alone to get on with my sorry life.

Daddy's belongings were shipped home. They had not even had the decency to bring them to the house. My mother had to go down to the docks with a friend on a cold, wet November morning to collect them. My father had died the month before. She had been forced to stand there and watch his beloved mandolin being carried down the gang-plank. His luggage had been dumped into her arms and she had been obliged to get a taxi home. She said her heart felt like it had been broken in two.

My mother hung up his navy blue uniform and I sneaked into her bedroom and took hold of one of the arms. The gold braids felt rough on my cheek. The smell of his tobacco lingered. Mammy left his pipe on the mantelpiece and we would all take a sniff of it now and again. It is hard to forgive the Merchant Navy for the way they handled the situation. We held a lot of anger against them for a long time. Everything confirmed that the world was too cruel a place.

Mammy was never the same again. A lot of the fight went out of her. Unfortunately she focused even more on me, so that I felt more trapped and alone than ever. I loved her, even adored her, but giving up my freedom was a high price to pay.

We were each caught up in our own torments. I was her distraction from her own pain and the onus was on me to be who she wanted me to be. I gave in again and again to her demands. I was still not allowed to wash my own hair, or have a bath without her standing making judgments on me. It became so invasive yet it was all she had to focus on. I was her life. I had to make it better for her. My weight plummeted. She loved my thinness. She possessed my every thought.

"You are so beautiful now," she exclaimed with tears in her eyes.

I was too weak to protest. I didn't know how to fight back. I had lost so many battles in my young life. I decided to go along with whatever choices were made for me.

CHAPTER 13

SEVENTEEN
AND RARING TO GO

I went back to school that September a young woman and just had to get through my last exams. I played the part of the happy and rebellious teenager. My popularity had increased and I would lead my 'girls' around the school and tease the younger students. It was one of the hottest summers in the '70s and we would lie out in the grass at break times. My gang and I would tie up our shirts and expose our midriffs to the rays of the sun.

A new secondary school was being built. We would be long gone by the time it was finished but our interests lay in the workmen who patrolled the construction area. Their naked upper torsos never ceased to amaze us. We would lie in the long grass spying on their bronzed masculinity. I joined in with the giggles and the general comments. I did my best to be the most boisterous and noisy of the gang. But in my mind, I could see my dad in the garden, doing his chores, his upper body bronzed and strong against the red-blue sky. One of my brothers would be grumbling, handing him a hammer or some other tool. They were more or less assigned to helping him. Mammy and I would sit on garden chairs taking in the scene, my mother giving her opinion now and then.

"Paddy, try and get the..." Or "Would it not be better...?"

Daddy would turn around and grind his teeth and I would laugh inwardly.

But Daddy had gone and I felt I would never laugh inwardly again. I could laugh like the best of them on the outside. But the outside was not the real me, it was all an act.

Prom night came and went.

"You don't want to go to the debs' ball, do you?" my mother asked, her tone filled with rhetoric.

I was the only one who didn't go. After all, what boy would want to go with me? That night I sat on my bed dreaming of what it would be like to be collected at the house by a handsome young man with an orchid for my wrist. I already had chosen my dress in my mind. Deep down I knew I did not deserve to go. I was too ugly to be seen at the beautiful Gresham Hotel.

I could see the crystal chandeliers hanging heavily from the ceiling, catching the light. I could picture the wooden dance floor and glided over it with my tall boyfriend. We smooched very slowly to a love song and I hummed it to myself. My turquoise-blue dress flowed with me. It was the colour of the sea where Daddy was buried. I reached out for his hand but only grasped at empty space. I looked around my bedroom and saw no light. No hope. I begged Daddy to take me away from it all. My door opened and my mother stood there in the darkness. She said nothing and slipped away.

Later on my mother gave me a box of chocolates because she felt sorry for me. I ate them greedily and then hated her for giving them to me.

"Maybe you should have gone after all," she said to me, waiting for my reply. Her doubts were my confusion.

I slammed the door and cried until sleep embraced me. That night my dreams were all I had.

Something shifted inside me and I began to yearn to shout obscenities at my mother and tell her to get out of my life, but I didn't. I loved her too much. She was my guiding light, really the only one I had. We both floundered side by side. Each lost in her own grief. Neither having the words or strength to emerge from her sadness.

I did well in my final exams. Mammy was very pleased and my brothers teased me for being such a nerd. I got six honours. Enough for university.

"You'll be going to secretarial college in September, then Niamh," she asked, but it was not a question. I agreed with anything she suggested. It had been a long time since I felt any ambition or passion. My daddy had died. Anything that had ever been good about me had been buried in the deep sea alongside his rotting corpse. I tore up my hopes and dreams and my lists of what I wanted to be. They littered my bedroom like white snowflakes. I was a broken piece of nothing.

"Whiskey, Whiskey, where are you?" I stood at the front door, waiting for him to respond. There was an eerie silence, no barking. I saw him crawling up the driveway. I knew something was wrong.

"Whiskey, Whiskey!" I screamed.

I lifted him up onto the kitchen table. He looked at me for the last time, his right ear cocked as he breathed his last breath. Mammy had rung the vet. It was too late. He had been run over and had come home to die. My Whiskey, my friend was dead. I caressed the white star on his forehead for the last time. I felt nothing now. Everything good in my life had been taken away from me. His warm limp body smelled of our park walks, our life and now his death. His blood dripped methodically onto the kitchen floor. Its redness seemed to follow me. I blew him a kiss. My faithful friend and companion had left me. I asked Daddy to look after him.

My brothers buried him in the mountains.

"Niamh, you can't do any more for him. Whiskey is dead. Try and get on with your life. You have to enrol for your Secretarial College," Mammy said.

I walked down Orwell Road, in Dublin on enrolment day and knew I had a long road ahead of me. I wasn't interested in happiness. I never even considered that it may be an option. Besides, someone like me did not deserve to be happy. I deserved just to exist and whatever was dealt out to me, I would gladly take.

Two old spinsters greeted me at the old Georgian door.

"Welcome to our establishment. We will show you to your place," Miss O'Donnell said. She walked ahead of me with a noticeable limp. I learned later from the other students that she had a wooden leg.

"Here comes Peg with the wooden leg," Sanda warned us, if we were up to no good at lunch times.

I was frightened of the parquet floors, reminding me of bad times long ago. I was led into a room full of typewriters. Rows and rows of cold metal greeted me. I took my place before my allocated machine. Young women smiled or gave me a wave. I was in a grave of my own doing. I shivered inwardly at the white keys looming in front of me.

"Now young ladies, time to open your book at page number . . ."

Yet, keen to please Mammy, I excelled at everything I did, even the things I disliked. I hated typing with a vengeance, but I did it. I wrote songs in my head the entire time I was there, beating out their rhythm on the clacking keys until my fingers were sore. The click of the typewriters became my symphony.

Miss O'Donnell and Miss McMurrow were very fond of me. I was one of their best students.

"Niamh, you will make someone a great secretary. You excel in everything," Miss McMurrow's little mouth exclaimed. I kept my distance in case something happened to them. Everybody I loved seemed to have disappeared or died in my life. I loved them for their kindness and felt safe in their college.

"Niamh, I have just received a potential position for you in a local bank," smiled Miss O'Donnell.

I went home and sat in the darkness. The real world awaited me. I read the banking form and signed my name on the dotted line. I felt that I had sold my soul a long time ago but this time there was no going back. I wrote two words in my diary that day: GOODBYE NIAMH.

CHAPTER 14

TWENTY
ABROAD AT LAST

"I have booked to go to Greece with Janet and Joyce," I told my mother.

Silence ensued.

I was ecstatic. I would be away from all the control at home. Away from my mother's constant nagging and complaining. Away from the merchant banking office that I worked for.

The island of Mykonos loomed before us. We giggled and took in the beautiful whitewashed buildings against the azure sea. It took my breath away. The ferry docked. A part of me didn't want to get off the boat. We had had such great laughs on board. We had flirted outrageously with not only the crew but every red-blooded male on the ship. I went along with the other girls and was swept up in the excitement of it all. I was free from rainy Dublin for three weeks. I was free from everything that depressed me. I was exhilarated and the sun shone mercilessly down on us three pale Irish girls. Joyce and Janet ran ahead whilst I struggled with the luggage.

"Wait for me. Wait for me!"

By the time I had caught up with them, they had already arranged accommodation for us, a little apartment practically in the town itself. Our luggage was propped onto a small trailer and we hopped into the white van that had three wheels. I had to sit in front with the driver as there was no room in the back with the other two girls. I felt uncomfortable. He was a middle-aged Greek with the blackest moustache that I had ever seen in my entire life. But his weather-beaten face crinkled when he laughed and I relaxed a little. His broken English was hard to comprehend but I understood enough.

"You girls, from Ireland," he said. "Plenty boys here. Like Irish. Good girls."

Janet and Joyce laughed hysterically. I tried to but decided to look outside at the scenery instead. I hoped that Mammy would not miss me too much. She had stood at the door waving me off.

"Be a good girl now," she had said. "Don't let anyone put anything in your drink. Be very careful and lock your door at night. Ring me when you get there."

"I will, Mammy," I had replied. "Don't worry about me. I'll bring you back a nice present. I love you."

It was everything I had dreamed of. The apartment had a beautiful balcony overlooking the town square. We could walk to all the bars and discos. The boats lay just across the way ready to take us to all the little beaches scattered around the coast. The blueness of the sea made me feel closer to Daddy. I blew him a kiss and the wind carried it away. I wished that he could be here to see this lovely island. I was brought back to the present.

"Niamh, get that into you," commanded Janet, shoving a glass of Bacardi and cola into my hand. "We have to get ready to go on the town. Drink up, will you, sleepyhead."

We had bought the Bacardi at duty-free and drank the lot while getting ready to hit the town. I was not a drinker in any sense of the word. I hardly went out to pubs in Dublin. The girls were seasoned drinkers and kept filling up my glass. I started to feel more relaxed and to enjoy the idea of being in this exotic place.

I put on my new white camisole lace top and lace knickers. They felt so soft and new. I had bought white trousers and strained to close the top button. They felt a bit tight.

"Niamh, you're gorgeous. Jesus, I wish I had your figure. They'll be sticking to you like honey," slurred Jane. She forgot what she meant to say and we all giggled. It was something about bees.

"Joyce, you can borrow anything you like from me," I whispered. She did. I hoped that she would be careful with my black top. Mammy had bought it for me and it had been expensive.

Jane, short and dark, led the way. Joyce, tall and with her lovely auburn hair, followed suit. I dashed madly to keep up with them. I liked the relaxed feeling that I felt.

I was on holidays with fun girlfriends. I was going to have a great time.

The disco lights were mind-boggling. Their neon colours blinded us when we entered the dark room and I looked up and watched them, mesmerised. We were at a disco at the edge of town that had originally been a sort of cave. The trendiest people went there, apparently. We were trendy too. Janet, with her chestnut brown hair and big bust, and Joyce, with her red hair and skinny body. I was tall, slender and had blonde hair past my bottom. My mother would not let me get it cut.

We moved towards the dance floor. I loved the freedom of being able to move any way I liked. Mammy had said that I had no rhythm. I thought I wasn't doing too badly as I gyrated to the seventies' sounds. My white outfit looked even whiter in the lighting. The lights shone on everyone and anybody who had white in their clothing seemed to illuminate.

"Look at us, girls. We look amazing. This is the life," shouted Jane.

I had never seen such magical lights before. My white body moved to the beat and the girls moved off in another direction. I followed suit. I knew my long hair looked glorious in the white lights and wondered if anyone could tell how blue my eyes were. I was tall. I was slim, but I was afraid to be on my own. Janet and Joyce had been abroad before and Mammy had asked them to look after me.

"Don't you worry, Mrs O," Janet had giggled. "We'll look after her. You can count on us."

Mammy was not impressed by Janet's forwardness. I thought her very confident and wished that I was more like her.

"Niamh, are you on the pill?" Janet had asked before we left. "It's better to be on it before we go on holiday." I was shocked. I knew nothing about dating boys. I had no intention of having sex with anybody, ever.

Janet and Joyce had already wrapped themselves around two German boys. I waited in the shadows and some men approached me and asked me to dance but I refused. I was terrified. Suddenly I wanted to go home. I wanted to get back to Mammy and her bright kitchen. I decided to find a phone. I told the girls that I would be back in a minute and asked them to wait for me.

"Niamh, don't go ringing your mother, for God's sake. Have another drink." But I had to get to a phone to tell Mammy that I was okay.

The phone booth turned out to be outside the disco and the bouncer gave me a bright green stamp on my wrist which would let me back in.

"I'm off to phone my mother back in Ireland," I told him. "I'll be back in a moment."

"Do you have enough coins for the phone?" he asked. He seemed friendly enough.

"Shall I show you where the telephone is, lady?" he asked.

"No, you're all right," I said. "I spotted it on the way here. It's not far. But thank you."

He followed me anyway. Maybe he was keeping me safe? I teetered slightly on my new white high heeled shoes.

Two young men appeared out of nowhere. They were smoking and chatted to the bouncer. I was glad he had been distracted from following me and opened the heavy door of the phone booth.

"Hello there, Mammy, I'm here!" I said with a voice as jolly as I could muster.

"Well, isn't that grand!" she said. We chatted a little about the flight and the island. Mammy had never been abroad. Mammy had never been on an aeroplane. She was right to be concerned.

"Don't worry Mammy. I'm okay," I said before hanging up.

I stepped outside the booth. Before I knew it, the bouncer and his two friends had grabbed me and dragged me across the road to the beach. I could not scream. Hands went over my mouth. It was an isolated part of the beach, behind a big boulder and all I could see were shadows and heard shouting voices in Greek. It all happened so fast that I couldn't react as fast as I should have. My senses had already been dulled by the alcohol. I kicked out and screamed but rough hands were placed over my mouth to the point that I could hardly breathe and I was pinned down in the darkness. My clothes were quickly removed and my lace knickers torn from my body. The soft lace of my camisole top grazed my left hip. My breasts were bitten and spat on. I was raped repeatedly by these three young men. They shouted obscenities into my ears. I chose not to hear them.

"You are more than words, Niamh," echoed in my mind. An eery silence ensued. I prayed that it would all be over. I felt the sea spray on my face. I went to wet my lips. Was I nearer the sea now? Was the tide coming in? The sea tasted strange and I heard bursts of laughter. I wasn't near the sea. They had urinated on me.

"Not my mouth, not my song," I gagged and choked in the darkness and my assailants ran off down the beach, laughing in the distance.

That was the second time that I had had sex in my young life. I was barely out of my teens and had been brutalized and raped, twice.

I heard the nuns telling me, "You are a whore and a bad seed."

"They are only words, they are only words," Ronka's voice whispered.

I vomited the words out of my body until I had no strength left. I looked towards the sea. It would be so easy to disappear forever, I thought. Daddy will take care of me now. I walked towards the angry ocean, screaming and howling. But something stopped me. I knew that I could not do this to my mother. Mammy was waiting for me at home. I had promised that I would bring home a present for her. I cursed her for loving me. I cursed the sea for not taking me again. I washed my body and hair in the incoming tide. I screamed out to the unlistening world:

"I AM NOT A TOILET

DEAR GOD ALMIGHTY I AM NOT A FUCKING TOILET."

I brushed the sand off my damp, bruised naked body and reached for my white trousers and camisole, now brown and stained with sweat and sand. I could not bear to replace my new lace knickers, ripped as they had been by the dirty hands of my assailants. I remembered my pink rosebud knickers of long ago. I thought of darkness and of pain.

I went back into the disco. Another bouncer was at the door. Janet and Joyce approached me. Gloria Gaynor's "I will survive" blasted from the speakers.

"We are going off to another disco with the lads here," they said. "Are you coming?"

"Did you ring your mother? I hope you didn't tell her that we were drinking."

They hadn't even missed me. I must not have been gone that long.

"You're a whore and will always be," Mother Joseph's words echoed.

I went with them. I couldn't bear to think of the alternative. I placed yet another event into the deep recesses of my mind. My glass was filled readily and I drank until I had no sense of anything anymore.

As we were walking out of the disco, a young woman approached me. She asked me if I had seen her young companion. We had been talking earlier to the two German girls. Her chocolate brown eyes met mine. She reminded me of Ronka. I told her to get in touch with the local police immediately.

We heard later that there had been a number of rapes on the island.

"Phew, that could have been us," Joyce said.

"Luckily, it wasn't," I replied.

That holiday, I drank myself into oblivion and slept with countless men. They seemed to like me at least, these strange men. We spent our days lying on the beach and our nights lying with different men. My lean brown body was used and abused again and again. I feigned lust and pleasure. It was a powerful thing to have young men clamouring for me. They all said that I was a wonderful lover. I was the whore of Babylon after all. It didn't occur to me that they might perhaps be attracted to something else. Everywhere we went, I joked. I filled every disco with laughter. I danced on every bar in Mykonos. I drank until I nearly passed out. I told myself that I was having a wonderful time. I convinced myself that I was. Janet and Joyce were getting a bit worried.

"Niamh, go easy there," they said. "Your mother would go crazy if she knew that you were drinking so much. She'll blame us for leading you astray."

"Well, she's not here is she?" I replied. "She's not bloody well here."

A tall blond Danish boy took me by the hand. We had sex on the beach that night. It was the same beach where I had been raped. I wiped my tears and he went back to the disco. I lay in the soft sand until the sun came up. It was a beautiful sight and the orange horizon greeted me. I wrote my name in the fine golden sand and stabbed it with a small piece of driftwood.

"Niamh, stupid and a whore
Just came back for bloody more."

I hid my eyes from the sun and buried myself in sand, covering myself right over my head so I could neither see nor breathe. They found me in my soft bed of sand and took me back to the apartment.

"Jesus Niamh, we were worried sick. Anything could have happened to you."

I began to laugh and my hysterical cries echoed through the stonewashed apartment.

I bought my mother a beautiful statue of the goddess Venus. They wrapped it up in bubble-wrap for me and her long, long hair disappeared into the brown box that the shop assistant had found. I wished I could disappear too.

I went home tanned and beautiful. I never saw my partners in crime again. Janet and Joyce saw my behaviour as a reflection on them. They felt guilty that they had influenced me. They were only a reminder of what had happened to me, anyway. I never told them what had taken place on the beach. I never told anybody. I did go down to the Rape Crisis Centre in Dublin though for a check-up. I wasn't pregnant and hadn't caught any diseases. I was relieved and thanked God for protecting me. I felt so ashamed and confused, I asked the nurse if I could be sterilised.

"You're too young," she said.

I didn't want to ever bring a child into this world. I felt so dirty. I took Daddy's penknife and cut my groin repeatedly in the night with long swift strokes. The blood seeped into my white sheets. Mammy thought it was my period. The stained sheets were symbolic of my life. My blood was tainted with all that had happened. I didn't sing for a long time. My song had also been tainted.

The rest of my twenties blurred together. I became a social butterfly. I flew from boy to boy and my life was pretty promiscuous. The quest for love was always misunderstood by me. I expected nothing and in return, got nothing. I was grateful for any crumbs that I did receive.

I continued to let myself be looked after by my mother. I convinced myself that this was not such a bad life but deep down I knew that there had to be something more.

The vultures circled and swooped down and took what they could from me. My girlfriends used my car when they liked and borrowed money and the men took my body readily. My startlingly good looks attracted many a visitor and I sank into an abyss of one-night stands and destructive behaviour. I felt so dehumanised that I began to enjoy feeling devoid of emotion, numb. I lived a double life. The little girl at home. The *femme fatale* at night. It was sweet revenge on my mother.

I joined the 'Brendan Smith School of Acting' and

had night classes. I loved its ferocity and intensity and how it got me out of the house. The people were all playing roles. I fitted in very well with plastic types and ego-trippers. A lot of gays became my friends. I felt comfortable in their company. I drank profusely after classes and starred in many plays.

"Niamh, we're performing in the Oscar Theatre, tonight, isn't that great?" Dave waved his hands in the air. He blew me a very pouty kiss and swayed his hips.

I loved being cast in character roles. I never wanted to be the French maid or beautiful actress. I felt at home playing old women or funny, eccentric roles. I loved to hear the audience laugh when I appeared on the stage. Mammy didn't come to see any of my plays. I didn't need her criticism. I joined a 'Debating Society' and loved to play with words. There was a part of me that thought I could be good.

"Niamh, you have great debating skills. We are going to Oxford for a competition. We would love to have you on our team," Sean said.

I didn't go. The fear of failure was too great.

"Niamh, it's just as well. You wouldn't know what to do there," Mammy said.

She was right.

Little by little I destroyed myself. I didn't deserve a man's love. Integrity meant nothing to me. I was praised for my acting and kept my voice hidden away. I worried that if I did sing out loud someone would take that away from me too.

CHAPTER 15

TWENTY-SEVEN
LEAVING HOME

I woke up from my dream and reached for my bedside lamp. Mammy sat there, staring at me. I said nothing. She slipped out of my room. I had had enough.

I heard Daddy whisper to me in the shadows that night, "ABANDON SHIP, ABANDON SHIP."

After seven years working as a secretary in industrial banking my boss, Jim, encouraged me to take time off and find out what I wanted to do. He knew that I was desperately unhappy and restless.

"Niamh, for God's sake, go away for a while," he said. "There will always be a job for you when you come back. See if you can do something with your teaching English diploma or with your acting stuff. Try to find out what makes you happy. You are so creative, Niamh. Please do something with it."

Jim was one of the few people in my life who believed in me. I was given a two-year sabbatical. He understood me. He knew I was drowning.

I sold my car and two weeks later told my mother about what I'd done. I was so caught up in the idea of getting away that I didn't plan anything properly. I was flirting with the wind, which moved me in every direction. All I knew was that I was going to London with my friend, Jacqueline.

I sat on my overfull suitcase. I hesitated over taking my finger puppets. These were the little felt friends that I used to annoy Whiskey with. He used to go crazy when I put them on my fingers. I stuffed them into the half-closed zip. Daddy's old guitar was coming too. I couldn't leave that behind. I heard shuffling outside my bedroom door but ignored it. Turlough had come home for a holiday and I was so pleased he was here.

"Let her go, Mum. You have to let her go," he said to Mammy as I passed them on the stairs. Eoghan chose not to come out and witness the drama. He was in the living room smoking. I saw a blue haze as I passed. He didn't want to say goodbye.

The taxi drew up and I held my breath.

"Niamh, it's time," I said to myself.

Mammy was distraught. The taxi would take me away.

"Come back, Niamh," Mammy said. "I will give you the house. I will give you anything. Don't go."

"I don't want anything," I said. "I don't want the bloody house. I want to get away from you."

Mammy ran after the taxi and I grasped her hand through the half-open window.

"Mammy, I have to go. Please, let me go." She let go of my hand and I saw her walking back to the house, head held high. It wouldn't do for the neighbours to be witnessing any sort of drama in our household. I saw Turlough putting his arms around her and was grateful that he was there for her. It was a black day for us both. I looked back again and saw her face. She looked as though her world had collapsed around her. Guilt washed over me and I cried all the way to the airport.

The taxi driver moved uncomfortably in his seat. "Have a Polo-mint love, it couldn't be that bad," he looked at me through his rear-view mirror.

I blew my nose on my handkerchief. It was the one Mammy said was for emergencies. I gazed at the green snot on the beautiful little forget-me-nots. I started howling all over again. It was a long taxi ride that day.

The taxi driver helped me with my luggage and heaved a sigh of relief when Jacqueline came to greet me.

"You could rent her in for a wake," he pointed to me. He practically ran back to his car, to get away from my howling.

"Now, don't you be worrying, Niamh. Your mother will get over it. For God's sake, you're not a little girl any more. You're twenty seven years of age!" she exclaimed.

That made me feel worse and the tears kept on rolling down my cheeks until I thought that they had nowhere else to go. My bright red velvet top was damp and sweaty.

Jacqueline was a very finely built young woman with large grey eyes. She was struggling with her own luggage and tried to help me with mine. She gave up after a while.

"Jesus, Niamh, put a sock in it. We're going away for a good time, not a funeral," she snapped.

She started me off again! I thought of all the deaths in my life and I wailed all the way to the plane.

A young glamorous stewardess came over: "Is there anything I can do for you?" she inquired.

"I want to go home to Mammy, I made a mistake," I screamed.

"Would you ever shut up! You're making a show of us. You're a grown woman, for God's sake," piped up Jacqueline.

I felt other passengers' eyes on me and closed my eyes. I am really gone from home. Let the adventure begin. I slept until we landed.

Jacqueline's brother, David, and his wife Lyn had offered to put us up for a few months, while we found our feet. The vague plan was to find temporary work and save enough to further our travels. We could teach English whilst travelling through Europe. It sounded so exciting. I had marked out on the map all the wonderful countries we could see on our travels.

We arrived in suburbia. Jacqueline's brother lived in Surbiton, a village outside Surrey. It was a neat semi-detached house with two large lion heads attached to two posts on either side of the driveway. Jacqueline saw me looking at one of the lion's heads:

"David has illusions of grandeur," she chuckled.

Like his sister, David was small in stature. His large grey eyes looked even larger because he had a high pale forehead. Lyn had a prominent smile. She gave the impression that she was constantly smiling. She towered over her husband which made them look a little odd together. I ignored a gnawing feeling in my stomach and put it down to being hungry. I hadn't eaten after all for nearly twenty-four hours with all the upsets.

This was a new start in a new country. I had escaped Ireland and all its painful memories.

"Make yourself at home, girls!" said David expansively as he showed us the tiny kitchen, cluttered sitting room and pocket handkerchief patch of garden. "And if there's anything we can do . . ."

We all sat down to our dinner at the oversized dining table. David sat at the head of the table and the busy floral wallpaper made the room seem even smaller.

"Help yourself now, girls. You must be starving after such a long journey," Lyn said.

I did. I ate everything that was put in front of me and more. David raised an eyebrow to Lyn. I saw his gesture and my heart sank. I refused dessert.

As she was family, Jacqueline got the lovely en-suite bedroom, while I stayed in the guest room, which had just enough space for a single bed and a very large wardrobe. The wardrobe was vast and old, made of dark wood and dominated the room. Looking at it made me want to vomit. Yet I had no clue where these feelings came from. I couldn't remember what may have happened in my childhood, if anything, to make me react so strongly but whatever the reason I didn't dare open its doors. I decided to keep my clothes in my overstuffed suitcase on a patch of free carpet so small that I couldn't leave the lid open. The room was cold and musty and was the only place in the house without double-glazing. I shivered and tried to feel positive though my body tingled with foreboding. The room radiated unfriendliness. The Laura Ashley wallpaper brought up memories that lurked in the cobwebs of my mind but refused to come to the surface. They seemed determined to stay put, deep in my tortured soul.

I sat down on the bed and cried. I longed for Mammy's captive arms. I was sorry, I'd made a mistake. I wanted to go home. I wanted to telephone her desperately, though I knew I'd regret it.

"Don't ring her for at least a week, until you both settle down," Turlough had said.

Then David barged into my bedroom without even knocking.

"Now, Niamh, you can't use the kitchen before we've eaten and cleared away our dinner. And we'll have no men in the house after dark. No one staying over, of either sex and you'll not use our bathroom. You can use Jacqueline's. We vacuum every day and don't like loud music. Don't tell me you're going to play that guitar, and another thing, buy your own toilet paper . . ." The house rules went on and on and I stopped listening after a while.

"Yes, David," I said quietly and stared at the floor.

He stood in front of the overpowering wardrobe and I felt that two people were talking to me. The dark oak and his dark hair merged into one and I drifted away in my thoughts. Was Mammy missing me? Why did I leave her? What should I do?

"We like people to be tidy around here," I heard him say. "There are enough hangers in the wardrobe to hang up your clothes. I will come back and inspect the room later."

He turned on his heels and left. He may even have clicked them together and saluted. I was back in the convent all over again, being demonized by Mother Joseph. It had been very kind of David and Lyn to have me to stay and I would do as they said. I sang to myself as I tried to gather up the courage to make friends with the old wardrobe.

"Hang up your clothes and look away
Tomorrow is another day
Have to find work and be free as a bird
I am taking in every word."

Maybe the wardrobe would be kind to me today and not take me into his deep recesses. I opened the heavy door.

"Please may I hang my clothes in here?" I whispered, placing my hands into the darkness. Sweat began to pour down my back. I took deep breaths and continued to sing to the wardrobe until I felt calm enough to unpack at last. But once they were all safely swinging on the matching wooden hangers, I placed a chair against the large doorknobs to be safe. Night would fall soon and I didn't want to be called to a dark place in the middle of the night.

"Supper is ready, Niamh," Jacqueline called chirpily.

I went downstairs to face the new people in my life.

That was the last time I ate with them.

David and Lyn made my life a misery and I accepted it, as I always did. The whore of Babylon didn't deserve better. The whore of Babylon had to be punished. I had no privacy. Jacqueline had a new boyfriend. She was in the pub every night and then they'd come home and have very noisy sex in the bedroom next door.

I could only use the kitchen when they were finished with their dinner but they stayed there longer and longer and sometimes I couldn't start cooking until nine at night. I gave up and started taking cold meals in my room. My weight plummeted. Mammy would be glad to hear of that.

David's constant presence unnerved me. His dark shadow seemed to hang around and for many months I was terrified to open my door in case he was lurking outside. I sang silently under the covers every night and prayed that my father would hear me. Silence was my only friend.

"Cut out that racket . . ." Lyn would shout up the stairs. My gentle strumming of my guitar was also forbidden. I tried to ring Mammy as little as possible.

"Niamh, Eoghan has gone to Boston. He has a chance of a job there," Mammy said softly.

"It'll do him good Mammy. He'll do well," I answered.

I hoped that Eoghan would do well there. I felt a bit angry that he had left Mammy on her own. At the same time, I knew it was best for everybody.

Mammy's three precious children had all flown the nest. She was alone. I felt so guilty I wanted to go home. But something prevented me from doing so. It was a real dilemma.

I did temporary office work at a well-known insurance company. My boss seemed to be pleased with me. Willing and friendly, I always made myself available to do overtime while the other girls whined and never wanted to do anything. They called me 'Paddy'.

"Paddy will do this," they'd snigger behind their hands, before passing me the most boring job in the world. "Paddy won't mind doing that . . ."

I didn't care. I was saving to travel. Paddy was given more work than anybody else and did it. Paddy corrected everybody else's untidy mistakes. Paddy was well loved by the supervisor of the typing pool.

"Paddy, can you work tomorrow?" she would ask, stooping low behind my chair and speaking softly. "I know it's Saturday but the girls seem to have busy social lives. You don't seem to mind." Her hand rested on my shoulder and she gave it an almost imperceptible squeeze before tiptoeing away.

I didn't. Anything was better than going back to David and Lyn. Jacqueline had her own social life now and hardly ever invited me out with her. We passed each other like ships in the night. It didn't bother me really. Her boyfriend was smug and rough. His friends were not my type at all. It was better that way.

There were ten Caribbean girls in the typing pool and they were delighted that the boss had a new slave and the senior girls a new scapegoat. They'd suffered long enough. As the only Paddy in the pool, I bore it alone. Regarding me as one of them, some of the Caribbean girls took me under their wing and let me sit with them in the canteen. I was content to listen to stories about their colourful lives both in London and back home. I saw a little bit of Ronka in a lot of them. Their chocolate brown eyes and buoyant spirits did me good. I even went to a Caribbean night out with them and was the only white girl strutting her stuff. The black men who approached me terrified me for some reason, though I knew they were gentle and kind. I had never been in the company of so many dark people. In Ireland there had been very few foreigners. I loved their music because of the way its throbbing rhythms reverberated throughout my body and made me feel alive. I did not wait to be asked and was soon up on stage, singing a strange reggae song with the band.

"You have a black soul, Paddy," the lead singer told me in the few seconds of silence between numbers. The smile on his face indicated that this was a compliment, but I remained wary. Black was associated with evil and I'd spent long enough as the daughter of the devil.

When I rang Mammy I told her that I was doing very well, keeping phone calls short so she wouldn't hear how miserable I really was. I knew she missed me desperately but I couldn't bear to think about going back to my old life. Ever the warrior, I would soldier on. Alone.

I wrote to my two brothers regularly. They wrote back intermittently. I always was the writer, even when Daddy was alive. Mammy hated letter-writing. I would write the letters and she would put her name and a little note at the end. Turlough was doing very well in his deep-sea diving career and Eoghan had his own construction company. He was just waiting for his green card. I was happy for him. I always had a soft spot for my quiet brother.

After six months I'd enough saved to move on. I had applied for various jobs teaching English as a foreign language and had my hopes pinned on one in Spain. It fell through so when I met a few Irish girls in a seedy Irish pub in Clapham, I decided to go with them, wherever it was.

"Niamh, we're going to Greece. Come along with us. It'll be great fun," screamed Bridget over the boisterous crowd. The group of girls were younger than me but had so much energy and vitality. I was borne along on the wave of enthusiasm. We all raised our glasses.

"To Greece, where it all happens," we chorussed. I never even thought of my past in Greece. It was long forgotten and would stay that way.

David and Lyn looked relieved by the news and Jacqueline was enthusiastic for me. She was wrapped around her gawky boyfriend and gave him a big slobbery kiss on his fleshy lips. I was happy for her. She deserved to be happy. She definitely wouldn't be leaving. She could stay as long as she liked. That was perfectly clear. A brief feeling of envy fluttered in my heart but soon disappeared:

"You have a few outstanding bills here, Niamh, that have to be taken care of . . ." David rambled off so many things that I stopped him politely half way through.

"Firstly, I would like to thank you for your shitty hospitality and atrocious treatment of me. I'm leaving here now and I wish all of you a very happy, boring life." I threw a ten pound note at David's feet.

"This should cover any damages that I might have incurred," I said curtly. Then, I gathered up my red polkadot suitcase and old guitar and bolted for the door. I didn't turn round to see their reactions but I gave one of the lion's heads an almighty shove with my suitcase. He came crashing down on the minute lawn. In my haste however, I had forgotten to ring a taxi. I headed for the nearest bus stop, which was at least half an hour away. I ran like a mad hatter and sat down in the bus shelter, breathless and shocked by my outburst. I looked down at my colourful striped trousers and they trembled at the knees. The bus wouldn't be for another hour. I felt slightly relieved but terrified. I had escaped yet again and freedom was beckoning to me. But where would it take me this time? At that stage, I didn't care. I started to laugh, slightly madly. It was so long since I had laughed. I sounded almost hysterical. Nobody was around so I laughed like a wild witch, while tears ran down my face.

I was swaying in the wind. I had no idea if I was doing the right thing. For so much of my life I had been told what to do, to wear, to eat, I no longer knew my own mind. I was like a weightless astronaut reaching out for something that kept floating out of reach.

CHAPTER 16

TWENTY-EIGHT
BRIEF ENCOUNTER

The plane began its ascent and I looked out of the window and saw another country disappearing before me. I wanted to ask the pilot to stop and turn around and fly back to Ireland to visit Mammy.

"Mammy, I'm not visiting you before I go to Greece. I haven't got the time. I'm sorry," I'd said when I'd called to say goodbye.

There had been a silence on the other end of the telephone. I had to be strong and not give in. I had to keep on moving away from what was pulling me back.

"Niamh, are you having a vodka? We're all set for the big adventure," Eileen screamed at me from the other end of the plane.

The handsome young steward looked at me with raised eyebrows.

"Yes, I'll have a vodka and orange juice please. If you can't beat them, join them . . ." I mumbled to myself without conviction.

On the ferry from Pireas harbour, near Athens, to the Greek island of Paros, I longed to splash in the foam that sprayed onto the deck through the steel railings. Instead, I tasted the salty tears of the sea on my parched lips. The baking sun beat down on my bare shoulders. I enjoyed the feeling of being held captive by the sun, after all, I was used to being in the control of another person and it felt soothingly familiar. I rubbed on some suntan lotion and lay back on a plastic lounger to enjoy the rays.

I scrambled ashore with the other Irish girls. Despite being a few years younger than me, they were more worldly wise. I was only too glad to have their company on this new adventure. I started looking for employment as a nanny or English teacher, but the only work available was in restaurants and bars. But even then I was turned away. I blamed my shyness. I was afraid of anyone new, particularly men, and my hesitation must have put them off. Again I was the outsider and this time I was even further from home. I began to panic. Again, I doubted my motives. I'd gone to Greece on a whim. What had I been thinking? I was a talented secretary so why wasn't I making anything of myself? Mammy would have gone crazy if she had known what I was up to. I had lied to her and told her I was taking a teaching job in Athens. In reality I had left a reasonable job with a good wage in order to simply seek my fortune. I knew I was just running away in search of the end of the rainbow. No one had told me that we make our own luck.

Mary and Eileen, the cheekier of the bunch, took me with them to a lively pizza restaurant that played loud Greek music. The owner was called Stavros, a burly, dark gorilla of a man, with black curly hair and very hairy arms. His brown eyes stared at us as he explained the deal:

"You are nice girls. You can work for me for whole season, yes?"

"Ooh, yes," we answered, grinning at each other. It seemed we had struck oil.

"But I need a deposit," he looked at us sadly.

"Deposit?"

"Yes, many people, they say they stay all summer but then they leave. I will keep deposit to make sure you stay. Then I give back at end." His eyes crinkled at the edges. He seemed genuine.

"You give it back at the end of the summer?" We felt less enthusiastic now, but a job was a job, right?

"Yes! I am like bank," he chuckled. "I will save it for you, my lovelies. You will then have lots of money at the end of this season. Work hard and we will have no problems."

I handed over practically all my savings. It was eight hundred pounds sterling.

"You're having us on, you must be mad. You didn't hand over all your money, Niamh," Rita laughed.

"You weren't born yesterday. For God's sake, you're older than the lot of us," Bernie exclaimed.

I looked at them dumbfounded. They were right. I was stupid. I was used to giving and others taking. I was devastated. The other girls had done deals and only given a certain amount of their savings. I had been done yet again, bled and hung out to dry! The mist in my head became even mistier. It was better not to think at all.

We worked hard all right, seven days a week, eighteen hours a day. We were up at dawn to prepare the dough, then we had to bake it and serve tables until midnight. It was exhausting. Stavros would lean his heavy, hairy body against mine at every opportunity. And he made sure that we didn't get our tips, frisking us at the end of the night to make sure that we'd given him everything we had. The other girls seemed to find ways of hiding the tips. I was always caught off guard. The other girls would giggle behind his back.

"This is my money," he said. "You are being paid enough."

I asked him for my deposit back, or half of it because I wanted to leave. He suggested that I sleep with him and then he would consider it. I stood there with my mouth open. Nothing had changed.

"No, thanks," I said and walked out into the sunshine with very little money and a feeling of total desolation.

"Other girls will share your money now you're gone. They stay for rest of season. Will be very rich girls," he laughed.

Yes, they did stay and they effectively took my money.

"You left, like the eejit you are, so we benefit, that's only logical," piped up Bernie. I suppose she had a point. Everybody seemed to win around me. I looked at my reflection in the restaurant window. I saw a loser looking back. A downtrodden, disheartened loser.

I walked down to the beautiful blue sea and sat there for hours trying to make sense of it all but I couldn't. I wiped my tears on the shoulder of my tee-shirt and walked back to the seafront to start looking for new work. It didn't take long.

I found work in a small bistro owned by a lovely French couple called Emile and Pauline. They had two beautiful little boys called Bastian and Didier. They wanted somebody to help around the restaurant in the mornings and babysit the boys until the restaurant was closed. I took one look at the two small dark, mischievous heads looking in my direction and was absolutely sold.

"Niamh, will the kite go any higher?" Bastian shouted.

"We'll try, sweetheart," I said as I held on to the string with Didier.

I had bought them the colourful kite and the three of us were mad about it. We went daily to the beach and tried to fly it as high as possible. We would sit and wait for a little breeze.

"Niamh, *vite, vite,* the wind is coming," Didier ran as fast as his little legs would carry him.

We picnicked on the beach in the evening or ate in the bistro.

Sometimes to supplement my income, I would sell big juicy red slices of melon on the beach to the tourists. The boys would help me cut it and place it in the cool box Pauline had given me. It was a great success. I loved being outdoors and felt a sense of freedom for the first time in a long time. At last happiness seemed possible.

Didier had his arms around my neck and I felt uncomfortable. I was afraid to love him. He wouldn't let go. I held him and prayed that nothing would happen to him. His dark eyes would look up at mine. I prayed that he would have a wonderful childhood.

"Niamh, I love you very much and will marry you some day," he smiled.

Bastian got jealous and jumped on my legs and we all tumbled into the golden sand. I thought I could settle into this kind of life. I had a sort of family of my own. Emile and Pauline were good to me. They treated me as one of the family. I loved their little bistro with its bright blue and white gingham table cloths. In the evening, I would sit outside when the children were in bed. Pauline would join me. We drank red wine and watched the world go by.

"Niamh, you must come to France one day. You will love the life there. You are a girl of *joie de vivre*," she spoke softly. Her dark hair shone in the light of a small lantern. I loved the quiet life. I didn't have to visit the bars and discos. I saw the crowds falling out of the discos and bars, late into the night. I was happy to sip my wine and watch the stars.

"Niamh, we have to tell you something. We are moving back to France. It is not the life that we expected here. I will go on with the boys and Emile will follow ..." Pauline was telling me but I didn't want to listen. They were leaving me. My beautiful boys were going away. I was devastated.

I went down to the ferry to wave them off. I saw Pauline wiping her tears and the boys crying uncontrollably. I tried to keep strong for them. I decided not to wait until the ferry left.

It was too hard.

"Goodbye me little sweethearts, be good for Mammy and I will meet you in my dreams. I will blow you a kiss and the stars will bring it to Paris for you," I said to them. I walked away and didn't turn back. It was the best for everyone.

I went back to my apartment and outside was the big colourful kite, wrapped up in string. A little note was left for me by Didier ...'*Je t'aime toujours*'. It was written in green crayon and a sun was drawn over the 't'. My tears fell that night in an empty apartment. My happiness had been short-lived.

I found another job in a restaurant along the promenade the next day. Work was not difficult to find in the middle of the tourist season. Dimitrios and Sophie owned a fish restaurant. It was quite a contrast for me. But I had hardened to the idea that happiness would elude me, and I battled on.

And then one May evening, I met Lucas. I had been working in Parikia for nearly a year. Tess and Sue were English, and as this was their last day on the island we went out for a night on the town. They were seasonal workers and I went out regularly for a drink with them. They wanted an evening to remember. Tess took along her camera so that she could capture the night's activities. A plump, small young man approached us.

"May I make a photo for you?" he asked indicating that he could take a picture with all three of us in it.

I couldn't quite place his accent and that intrigued me. The more I listened to him the more his soft round features started to appeal to me and the more I realised he was attracted to me too. We started to chat and before we knew it, it was very late indeed. Lucas was charming, intelligent and self-confident and within a few hours he had stolen my heart. Unfortunately, like Tess and Sue, he too was leaving the next day so we exchanged addresses.

Lucas was leaving very early on the local ferry to Athens but I had a mad urge to say my goodbyes again and rushed down to wave him off. We embraced passionately and I felt more alone than ever as the ferry pulled out of the small port. I waved until he was a small dot on the horizon. The sun had come up and I walked with a heavy heart to the fish restaurant. I wondered if he would write to me. I was deep in thought when suddenly I heard a shout. It was Dimitrios.

"You stupid girl, you are late! I will take money from you for this."

Dimitrios was a small, heavy-built Athenian and his wife was a small frail islander called Sophie. He terrorized her and all the staff. Sophie and I would stay at the back of the kitchen peeling potatoes. We would place one of the big restaurant tables in front of us so that we would be invisible to the boss. This seemed to work and mostly he would forget that we were there. When Dimitrios was on the prowl my hands became clammy and I was overcome with nausea. I could sense the impending doom.

He flew into a rage about how slowly we were working that day and to prove a point he thrust the sharp blade of the knife he held in his hand downwards with such force towards the head of the swordfish he was preparing for the oven that its head flew through the air and landed at my feet. The crimson blood formed pools around my new pink flip-flops. The swordfish's eyes looked up at me beseechingly. I was heartbroken for him. His beautiful long sword had broken off and was now detached from his jaw. The jagged edge had missed my toes by inches. My white t-shirt was splashed with pieces of jelly-like brain. I sang softly to myself.

"The snow-white princess and the unicorn were sad today

But we will come back to fight another day"

I stepped silently out of the slime that was coagulating around my feet, picked up the severed head and sword and walked out to the pier and threw them into the sea. I heard Dimitrios roaring with laughter and shouting at me to come back immediately. I didn't. I just kept on walking.

The next day I found another job in another restaurant. Janos was tall and dark and wore a large hairy moustache. He was very talkative and his eyes roamed constantly up and down my body. His wife, Ella, hated me and gave me the hardest jobs to do. But I had to stay. I needed the money. Ella pinched me every time I went near her.

"You are a whore, you foreign bitch," she would spit at me, reaching out to twist the flesh on my arm until it was black and blue. I didn't care. I stopped feeling that sort of pain a long, long time ago. Pain was not important. I had to focus on my future.

The one beacon of light in those dark days in the sunshine was to think about my brief encounter with the charming young Dutchman called Lucas. He wrote his first postcard to me from the airport travelling back to the Netherlands. I held it to my heart and kissed it. Somebody out there cared for me.

We wrote to each other constantly for five months on thin blue airmail paper folded into three. Rather than lick the flap of the envelope to seal it, I would smother it with kisses. Over the next few months we got to know each other through our writing. Lucas was an engineer and worked at a nuclear power station in the south of the Netherlands. He told me his daily routine and I told him mine. We wrote lyrical poetry to each other and we both longed to see each other again. In October he came back.

I waited for him at the port, dressed in white and feeling as if I was a bride waiting for the groom to come home.

We spent a wonderful two weeks together.

"Let's go to another beach today and take a picnic," Lucas said.

"And I can show you more of the island," I replied contentedly.

We hired little scooters and went to the other side of the island. Paros is not a big island. We stopped at a small fishing village called Aliki and watched the fishermen repairing their nets in the blazing sun. Later, we sat at a lovely little tavern eating calamari and drinking Retsina wine.

"We will halve the bill," said Lucas.

I handed over my two hundred drachmas. I felt a little twinge. But he was right. I always paid my way. It seemed unromantic though. Lucas put the money in his little black leather purse, which had a thick silver chain attached to it. It disappeared into his pocket. He would calculate what we spent every day and we would always split the difference.

We spent days lazing in the sun and nights making love. I felt I was on another planet. Lucas was easy to talk to and had travelled extensively. He painted a colourful picture of his life as a bachelor in the Netherlands. I envied his confidence and easygoing manner.

"Niamh, it's not practical to have a relationship with somebody in another country. Would you consider coming over to the Netherlands and working there?" he asked one day.

"I'd love to!" I replied enthusiastically.

I couldn't believe that somebody would actually ask

me to their country. I looked at Lucas' blue eyes and I knew that I had fallen in love with him. He was so kind to me. He accepted me as I was. We never discussed our pasts. He would be my future.

"I'll follow you over. I want to finish up my work here and sort things out," I said.

I wanted to finish my contract and get the money that was owed to me. Stavros was not the only one to be 'a bank'. Janos owed me several weeks' wages at this stage, including a lot of overtime. The restaurant was very quiet at midday. It was siesta time and I had to clean the kitchen. I decided to approach him.

"Janos, you know I'm leaving in a few days for Athens. Please, could I have the money that you owe me? I have written down the hours to make it easier for you," I said nervously.

"You always good worker, Niamh. I like you very much," Janos said grinning broadly and looking around as if there was somebody behind him.

He suddenly started caressing my cheek and his hands lingered on my breasts. His brown bulging eyes met mine.

"Janos, leave me alone please. I'm only asking you for the money that you owe me," I said with a slight panic in my voice.

"Maybe we come to an arrangement. You like your boyfriend? Does he do nice things to you?" His hand slipped down to the silver button on my white shorts. I slapped his hand away and was terrified. I thought of Lucas waiting for me. I wanted to go to the Netherlands as an independent woman. Lucas had been perplexed that I had no savings.

"You are twenty nine and have no savings in Ireland. I find this very strange," Lucas had commented and looked at me suspiciously. He was right. I would ring Mammy and ask her if she'd put money away for me. I had to prove to him that I could support myself. I didn't want him thinking that I was a gold digger. Janos grabbed me by the waist and pulled me towards him.

"You have to do something nice for me for your money," he whispered into my ear. I felt his hot breath all over me and his trembling hands started unzipping my shorts.

I heard a scream and opened my tear-filled eyes.

"You whore, what you do with my husband?" Ella was standing there. I was so relieved! She screamed hysterically and pushed her husband away from me. She slapped him hard on his face. He stumbled out of the kitchen.

"I AM NOT A WHORE. Janos won't give me my money," I screamed back at her. "I only want my money. It's my money." I was getting more hysterical. She slapped my face hard and went to the cash drawer. She took out hundreds of drachmas. She threw the bundles onto the floor. I crawled on the floor and picked up each note individually then counted them one by one. I clasped my money to my heart and blew kisses up to the ceiling to my shining prince in the faraway land. I thought of the fantastic life ahead of me. I dreamt of happiness. I dreamt of peace and love. I thought that the Netherlands would free me from all the dreadful events that seemed to follow me. I ran out of the restaurant, clutching my money and never looked back. I was free. Immediately I rang Mammy to tell her that I was in love.

"I hope to God that he is not a pimp who will put you in a window with a red light," she said.

"Mammy, don't be so suspicious. Lucas is an engineer. He's kind to me and we love each other. I am going to follow him to Holland because I love him and that's that," I said.

Oh sure, I laughed to myself, but part of me was apprehensive. I really didn't know this man. I was going to another country, to a different culture and to somebody that I only knew through writing and a two-week holiday. I felt a shiver running down my spine. I ignored it. I knew I was making the right decision. He was so sweet to me and educated.

"Education is the key to knowledge. Knowledge is power," Daddy had explained to me. Educated people were civilized people. I knew Lucas. I knew him. I convinced myself that I was doing the right thing and looked forward to a new adventure. I left Paros by ferry. It had been my home for almost two years. I waved to the little windmill as it disappeared in the distance. The wind was quite cold and I wrapped two sweatshirts around my shoulders. I would have to get the bus in Athens. It was a night ferry and I counted the stars in the dark night. Would Lucas be counting the days before I came? How many stars would bring me closer to him in his country? I counted until I fell into a deep sleep.

I chose the cheapest way to get to Amsterdam. It was the 'magic bus' route. This was the cheapest way to travel through Europe.

"Niamh, it's the cheapest but don't expect luxury for the price," Graham had sniggered. He was always smoking weed so I gathered that he was just on another high. The bus would pass through Italy, France, Germany and Belgium and would deposit the passengers in Amsterdam. I learned later that the 'magic' bus got its reputation from the bad driving of the exhausted drivers and the general conditions in the bus. It was the 80's and the safety legislations were not tightly enforced in Greece at the time.

"It's called the 'magic' bus because it will be a bloody miracle if you get to your destination in one piece," Rolf told me. He was a seasonal German worker who had come back to Greece for the past decade. He proceeded to tell me of all the accidents that had taken place over the years. He found the whole situation very funny indeed.

"Thanks a lot, Rolf. Thanks for the vote of confidence," I had said, a little bit alarmed. I had no choice now. I had booked and paid for the trip.

"I'll be there on the 22nd," I said lovingly into the phone.

"I'll be waiting," said Lucas, and it sounded the most wonderful thing in the world. Somebody would be waiting for me. Just me. Only me. He would ring up the station nearer the time to know when I was definitely at the Amsterdam station. It was October and the tourist season was over in Paros. Winter was approaching.

I looked around at the other passengers. They were an unkempt bunch of travellers. Most of them were students or veteran season workers. I saw Petra, a young skinny girl whom I had seen around Paros. She had also worked for the season there.

"Hi Petra, where are you going?" I inquired.

"I hope to get to Amsterdam. There's a job waiting

for me there," she replied. At least I now had someone to talk to for the trip. We sat next to each other on the old, dirty bus. The seats creaked sadly as we sat down. We both burst out laughing. The bus started filling up with all sorts of dishevelled travellers.

A microphone cackled: "Hello, I am Manos and I hope to bring you on a safe journey to your destination. I ask you one thing. I am fast driver. I not make many stops for toilet. It a waste of time. You good to Manos, I good to you. No trouble, no problem." Manos was clearly used to saying this over and over again. His voice had a metallic sound to it as if it was a computerized recording. His small sturdy body faced the passengers aggressively.

The bus smelled of cigarettes and dirty clothes. I had just one rucksack, which I had purchased for the trip. My suitcase had been too battered and torn. I looked down at my brown feet in my Jesus sandals. They were feeling the cold now. I had sold my cowboy boots to a young German tourist. She had admired them and extra money was always welcome. My Swatch watch, jewellery and other articles of value had also been sold for the 'Amsterdam fund'. I regretted selling my purple woollen jacket. It would have made a nice blanket in the freezing bus. The heating system was out of order and we all shivered uncontrollably. I wanted to be financially independent until I got a job in the Netherlands. I wanted to make Lucas proud. I longed to see and touch him. I settled in for the journey to begin. Petra and I huddled together and I was grateful that she shared her warm sleeping bag with me. I tucked it in under my frozen toes.

"Nighty night, don't let the bed bugs bite." I whispered to Mammy, so many miles away in Ireland.

I dozed off.

"Manos, wake up, Manos, you bloody idiot, wake up." Two English lads were shouting at our driver. He had fallen asleep at the wheel and we had started to sway to and fro on the highway. We all decided to take it in turns to sleep from then on. Somebody would have to watch the driver. He drove right through Italy up to Paris. The driver that was to replace him never turned up, so one of the passengers pitched in. He was a big Swede called Bo who would sometimes take the wheel. It was quite hairy at times. We stopped infrequently at little cafés along the way and toilet stops, more often than not, were at the side of the road. Most of the passengers didn't have the money to be eating at restaurants. We preferred supermarkets.

"Manos, 'eatey-eatey'. We want to buy some 'eatey-eateys'," John shouted. He was an extremely funny Irishman with a generous nature. He shared what he had with the more needy. We christened him 'Robin Hood'.

"Wee-wee stop now. Five minutes," Manos declared at last.

We all fell out of the bus and the girls relieved themselves in a row down one side of the bus and the boys did the same on the other. If we needed to do rather more, then we had to wait until there was a green patch at a later relief spot. I decided not to eat so that I wouldn't have to deal with the discomfort and embarrassment. That wasn't hard to do. I didn't want to waste my money on buying food plus the fact was that I had forgotten to exchange money into different currencies. Each country in Europe had a different currency then. Petra and I lived on re-filled tap water in our plastic bottles. Now and again, a cracker or piece of bread was offered to us, but I declined. I wanted to be beautiful for Lucas. The thinner I was, the better.

It was a real community, our little bus. Despite the cold and hunger, we had great laughs and our motley crew of dishevelled travellers shared stories of our travels.

"When I was in India, they thought I was a guru . . ." Or "The girl couldn't get enough of my English charms..." Every story was hilarious because the damp smell of sweat and unwashed bodies had another tale to tell.

I scratched my head, yet again. Petra was scratching her head and turned to me. Hans, the long-haired German behind us was also scratching regularly.

"Niamh, I think I saw something moving on your head," Petra exclaimed.

We had new little friends in our bus. My long blonde hair was a colony to lice. The bus was infested. I couldn't believe it. When would I ever reach my Prince Charming? I closed my eyes and wept.

"Only dirty children get lice. It will never happen to you," Mammy had explained. Now I believed her.

We reached Munich in one piece. Twenty of us waited for a new bus to take us to the Netherlands, through Belgium. Our group was getting smaller. We waited five hours in the cold and rain. German passersby stared at the unruly young people shivering from the cold. I tried to ring Lucas but got no answer. I left him a message.

I arrived at Amsterdam Central Station, dirty and exhausted. It was freezing and all I saw were dark clothes and grey skies. It was such a contrast to blue-and-white Paros. I felt my mood changing and started to panic.

"What if he doesn't come to meet you?" Petra asked.

"He will, he will. He has to." I had blind faith that he would.

I saw nobody there at first but then saw a figure approaching me. It was Lucas. He looked different. The last time I saw him he was tanned and bright. Now, he stood there dressed in gray and looking so pale. It took my eyes a few seconds to recognize him and then I threw myself in his arms.

"Lucas, it's you, Lucas. I'm here," I cried.

My prince was waiting for me. He had waited nine hours, since there had been so many delays. He embraced me tightly and I didn't want to let him go. I couldn't believe that anybody would wait for me. I loved him unconditionally from that moment. I was determined to be everything he wanted me to be. I would learn the language, learn everything. I was going to be the best that I could be for him. Because he loved me and who could love somebody like me? I would die trying. I would.

Lucas' car was warm and I felt safe. I didn't care that I looked like a dirty hippy. Lucas didn't seem to mind. I just wanted a long, warm shower and something to get rid of my little friends. We stopped off for petrol on the way to his home.

"Lucas, may I have a Mars bar please?" I asked shyly. I hadn't eaten for five days and nights.

"Lucas, can we stop off at a drug store? I need to buy some special shampoo for my hair." I never did tell him what sort of shampoo I needed. I was too ashamed.

I did learn the Dutch language. I went to a day school, twice a week and was fluent within three months. Lucas put yellow stickers on the fridge to remind me not to speak English. He wrote sentences on them, such as:

"You have to speak the language to know the people" or 'You want to know what my mother says about you." I was happy that he was so helpful. I embraced everything that was Dutch. His family seemed very friendly. His mother had been recently widowed. She was a big country woman with no English. She had great difficulty accepting a foreigner into the family at first.

"Niamh, I'll go there without you this time. She has to get used to the idea that I met a foreigner," Lucas explained. It was all too much for her.

"I understand," I said and waved him off. Something told me that I would have to work at being accepted by his family. A familiar feeling of rejection and inferiority crept through my body. I shivered and went inside. I found a mouldy packet of peanuts and crammed them into my mouth. The salt made me gag. I sat and waited opposite the cheap white plastic clock on the wall. It ticked the silence away from my beating heart.

Then the day came that I had to meet his whole family at his mother's house. I was determined to make the best of it for Lucas sake.

I may have been a foreigner but I also happened to be Catholic. I hoped this fact would not be stacked against me. From the moment I met his mother it was clear that she was trying her best. So I would do my best too. His two sisters, one of them married, and his brother were all very hospitable. But it was all very formal and different. Three kisses were plonked on my cheeks. I just wanted a hug. I didn't understand this kissing business. I didn't like it.

"Welcome to the Netherlands," his brother, Art, said.

The whole family looked me up and down and took me in. His mother was the most critical. I sat there with my hands on my lap. I felt like I was back in school. I was in a fish tank and everybody was looking at me. I never got rid of that feeling with his family. Their little gestures or eye contact with each other spoke volumes. I always felt excluded although they seemed to be kind. Nothing was ever said but it was the subtleness of their behaviour that irritated me. I could never put my finger on it. I lowered my head. I felt so uncomfortable, the strange language being spoken and shy smiles directed at me. I had worn a skirt for the special occasion. Lucas had ironed it for me. The pleats were quite complicated. I hadn't ironed in years. In Paros, everything was just taken off the line when it dried. Lucas had lived on his own since he was eighteen. He was very self-sufficient.

"I'll show you how to do it. You'll have to get used to it anyway," Lucas said.

Lucas could do anything. I felt inferior.

"My mother was impressed with what you wore," Lucas said later on the drive home. I looked down at my long pleated skirt and gaudy top.

I would get used to their ways. I would try to be more Dutch. It was important to Lucas. He seemed different in their company. I was Catholic, they were Protestant. Lucas had been brought up in a sober, frugal way. He was from a simple, hardworking family with deep belief in the bible and Church on Sunday. I was a city girl with a generous and big-hearted family. We didn't have a good reputation with saving money. We liked nice things. I hated churches of any kind and usually said whatever came into my head. Lucas thought about what he said first.

Lucas' mother never understood my jokes, and she disliked my red lipstick and long hair.

"Would you not get your hair cut?" she said. "It looks so untidy."

"What's that black stuff on your eyes?" she exclaimed. It was my eyeliner. Lucas's sisters never wore make-up. His married sister's children didn't want to kiss me because they were afraid of my lipstick. I had to do better. I stopped wearing lipstick and eyeliner.

"What are they on your feet?" Can you walk on them?" I know she didn't mean any harm but I stopped wearing high heels and started wearing flat shoes.

"Flat shoes are for women with no style or ambition," Mammy had said. But I wanted them to feel comfortable with me.

That Christmas, Lucas and I flew home to meet Mammy in Dublin. I had on a black and white cheap winter coat, flat shoes and a very decent black jumper. Mammy took one look at me at the door. She had not seen her daughter for nearly three years.

"Jesus Christ, I hope the neighbours didn't see you. Look at the state of you." She raised her hands in horror. "Where is he, then?"

Lucas was behind me. He stepped forward to introduce himself.

"Jesus, he's a leprechaun. A bloody leprechaun."

Lucas thought it was a joke and laughed nervously.

He wasn't a very tall man. I explained to him that Mammy had a sharp tongue.

"He's a face on him like a bowl of porridge," Mammy whispered to me later. I thought that was a compliment, coming from Mammy. Lucas had beautiful skin. But she soon changed her tune when she heard that he had a very good job as an engineer and had extremely good prospects.

"Welcome to the family, Lucas. I'm going to make you a big fry-up." She did so. I was told to have a cup of tea instead.

"Niamh, you have a big arse on you there. I hope to God you're going to do something about it." I didn't take offense. I was in love. Nothing could touch me now.

Mammy gave her blessing and Turlough and Eoghan were home for Christmas and took Lucas out on the town on Christmas Eve. I stayed at home to help Mammy with the preparation for the Christmas day dinner. We chatted excitedly in the bright, warm kitchen.

"Niamh, I want you to be happy," she said. It was the nicest thing she had ever said to me. I knew she meant it. Mammy approved of Lucas. She could see that I was a success at something. Lucas got on with Mammy. Everybody was happy.

I couldn't find decent work in Vlissingen, the Dutch village in which we were living, so I worked as a chambermaid by day in a big hotel on the promenade. It was called Hotel Bos but it was quite rundown and the 'o' and 't' had disappeared from the sign. So, I went to work at the Hel Bos every day. I had to learn my Dutch and my fellow maids would teach me all the curse words in the Dutch vocabulary.

"Niamh, say '*neuken in de keuken*', Carla said. She was a tall and gangly with a very boisterous laugh. She told me that it meant cooking in the kitchen. I repeated it to Lucas, later that night. He was not impressed. It meant something totally different! But I enjoyed the simplicity of the work and the frolics of the other girls. I loved to cycle down the promenade every day and feel the sea breeze in my hair. I considered myself to be very lucky indeed. At night, I cleaned offices. I was collected by a big white van at the end of our road and worked from 5.30 until 9.30. I would chirpily clean different offices in an industrial area outside the town. I had to prove to Lucas that I was not taking advantage of him financially. I was independent. I would hand over my wages to him to put towards the costs of running the household. That only seemed fair. I trusted him with that sort of thing.

"Niamh, I have made a list of shopping that has to be done. Try to speak Dutch as much as possible. It's the only way that you will learn the language," Lucas advised.

"I will and thanks for all your help," I smiled and wrapped myself around him. I wrote little notes in his lunchbox telling him that I was thinking of him.

He was my rock. Lucas guided me and told me what to do.

What would Lucas think of this? What would he do in this situation? I could hear his deep voice giving me his fatherly advice. That's what people do when they love you. They make decisions for you and know what's best for you. Mammy knew what was best for me. So did Lucas. I was very lucky indeed!

"Niamh, I have an old pair of hiking boots that you can borrow. You don't have to buy winter boots. They are too expensive," Lucas said.

He was right. We had to save money and I handed over my Christmas bonus to him for our saving fund.

CHAPTER 17

THIRTY-TWO
HONEYMOON

We lived together for three years before deciding to marry. Mammy had been putting the pressure on.

"Niamh, you have been sharing his bed now for three years. It's time that he asks you to marry him," Mammy said over the phone.

I started thinking about what she said. Why didn't Lucas ask me to marry him? What was stopping him? We got on great together. We had moved up to Dordrecht, a small town just south of Rotterdam. I had a good job too now, in an academic publishing company. My Dutch was fluent. I decided to broach the subject. I was trembling because maybe he didn't want to take the relationship a step further.

"Lucas, I was thinking about our time together. Mammy was saying that she found it strange that we are living so long together and we haven't taken it a step further," I stammered.

Lucas looked at me. I knew this look. He never spoke until he had thought about what he should say. There was a long silence and I held my breath.

"Niamh, in the Netherlands, we live together for quite a while. There's no rush in getting married. However, I will consider it and get back to you," he said, and two weeks later he did.

"Would you like to get engaged?" he asked.

I was over the moon. We got engaged in Paris. It was the most romantic weekend I had ever had. We stayed outside Paris on a camping site, which was cheaper. But Lucas had bought an expensive ring after all. He asked me to marry him on the Champs Elysées. I was bursting with love for him. Lucas was the love of my life.

Six months later, we went to India for three weeks. I loved the elegance of the small women wearing their colourful saris. I felt like a giant clumsy fool amongst them. We had decided to get married in India whilst on holiday but when we heard that it would take longer than usual to get a marriage licence and that perhaps it wouldn't be officially accepted in the Netherlands, we changed our minds.

"Let's take a little bit of India back to the Netherlands with us," I exclaimed. I chose a beautiful green and pink sari and felt its smooth texture against my cheek.

"Yeah, why not?" Lucas agreed and we spent two hours bargaining down the price in the sari shop. Lucas drove a hard bargain.

We travelled to New Delhi, Jaipur, Udaipur and I fell in love with the sounds and smells of India. The Taj Mahal beckoned to me and I sat with Lucas taking in its overpowering beauty. I held his hand and never wanted to let it go. How could I possibly be so happy? A slight cloud of doubt hung over me.

"You will never be anything. You are a nothing," Mother Joseph's words ran through my mind.

Eoghan had been working in Boston, USA, for a couple of years by then. He had a hard time trying to get a Green card and was now at the end of his tether. It was all very vague on the telephone. It appeared that he had had his own building and construction company and he had gone bust. The strain was too much for him. Eoghan was two years older than me but we always had a bond, despite our upbringing.

"There's plenty of work here, Eoghan," Lucas had said to him with genuine enthusiasm when he had telephoned us one windy Sunday.

Little did we know what that invitation would entail. Ten days later Eoghan arrived from America. We collected him at the airport. I hardly recognized him. He was thin and frail with a large gap in his front teeth. He had inherited my mother's weak teeth but had always had caps on them. He had somehow neglected to replace them. He looked disorientated and clutched his grubby rucksack to his chest. I couldn't believe that this was my brother.

"We'll fatten you up, that's for sure," I heard myself saying.

Eoghan clung to me like a safety line. I inhaled the smell of his unwashed clothes and knew something was terribly wrong.

He would stay with us until he got on his feet. Lucas helped him to find a job as an administrative worker through an agency. Then he organised an apartment for him to stay in that was not too far from us and not too far from his job. He would stay with us until the apartment was ready. Eoghan came at a very busy time in our lives. We were planning our wedding and he stayed with us from January until May. Things seemed to be looking up for him. We were so busy organizing the wedding, however that Eoghan's health was not a priority for us.

Lucas got caught up in the arrangements for the marriage. He handled it like a military operation. Nothing could go wrong on our day. His family wanted to organize everything.

My mother originally refused to come to the wedding. She was terrified of flying. Yet by this time I had not seen her for a year.

"You can come along with Turlough," I pleaded. He'll look after ye, Mammy."

"No, Niamh, I'll not come and that's an end to it."

"Mammy, if you don't come to my wedding, you will never, ever see me again!" For the first time in my life I decided I was standing firm. It was a harsh statement to make, but I was determined to win this battle. I was going to have a fairytale wedding in a 10th century cathedral in Dordrecht and both our families were going to share a fantastic day with us.

I walked down the aisle like a real princess. My green and pink sari shone brightly in the vast chandeliers. I saw Mammy, supported by Turlough and Eoghan, and felt a temporary pain in my heart.

"Daddy, if only you were here today to see your golden princess, if only . . ." I wiped away a tear as Lucas approached me.

"*Ja, Ik wil. Ik wil met jou trouwen,*" I answered and I meant it with all my heart. Lucas and I looked at each other and we loved each other. His eyes were bright with held-back tears. I would never disappoint him. He was my knight in shining armour.

The sun shone beautifully for a May wedding. We all clambered aboard a boat to have a buffet lunch and sail around the area and outside Dordrecht. Mammy seemed very happy and even Lucas's Mammy dried a tear. Our twenty-five guests joined us for a beautiful dinner in the Hotel Bellevue in Dordrecht. We cut a three-tiered cake full of pink and white roses, high up in the hotel's dome.

"Mammy, are you happy?" I asked.

"Niamh, I am. I know now that somebody can look after you when I'm gone," she replied.

Lucas and I were committed to each other now. We had been married in a church ceremony before God and the congregation.

Lucas and I decided to return to Paros for our honeymoon. I looked out at the port as the ferry docked on that scorching hot May day and felt sick. Bad memories were part of this island too, even in beautiful Parikia. It was the place where I had worked, the place where I had been forced to beg for what was rightfully mine and the place where I had fallen in love.

We spent our days lazing in the sun, having cocktails in our little bar overlooking the bay, and making love in our pension under the bright stars. A lot of changes had taken place since I had worked there. I saw some familiar faces and greeted them. I avoided the restaurants that had treated me badly. But some of them also had changed hands. Parikia was getting bigger and more touristic. It was three years since I had left the island. The beaches were the same and our long beach walks hand-in-hand made me feel safe and loved.

Back home in our sixth floor flat in the small town of Dordrecht, Lucas and I were very much the honeymoon couple. I would do everything I could to make him feel happy, loved and comfortable. I'd visit a range of shops every day to buy the freshest vegetables and meat and clean the house daily while he was out at work. My family and my childhood troubles seemed far away. Eoghan was soon to move out and things were going well for him too. It was a small town with lots to do. My job was only temporary but they had promised me a permanent position if something came up. I was confident that that would be the case. I did my work very well and was a hard worker. I was settling in really well. We were looking forward to lots of happy years ahead.

"Niamh, you are happy at last," I said to myself in the hall mirror. I felt good, and loved being loved.

But four weeks after we came back from our honeymoon, things went very wrong.

Eoghan rang me at work one morning. He sounded very down.

"Niamh, I am very tired and I took a half day off work. I don't want to go back there."

"Eoghan, I'll tell you what. I'll come home early and get some cream cakes on the way. How about it? We can talk further then. See you soon," I put down the phone and asked my boss if I could go home early. I phoned Eoghan before I left to tell him I was on my way. Nobody answered. I felt a sinking feeling in my stomach. I ignored it. As always.

I pushed open the door and walked into our apartment. It was quiet. The balcony door was open but I presumed he'd wanted some fresh air. There was no sign of my brother. I called out. Desperation engulfed me. I saw a bible open on the settee and ran towards the open door of the balcony. This couldn't be happening!

At first I saw nothing, then I looked down at the street below and saw a half dressed figure lying bloodied on the pavement. In the distance I heard sirens.

"Eoghan, Eoghan, Jesus, Eoghan. What have you done?" I screamed at the top of my lungs, then I grabbed my handbag and ran down six flights of stairs to wait for the ambulance. In my panic, I forgot that there was a lift. I held Eoghan's hand and prayed that he was okay. Blood dripped from his mouth. It dripped onto my blue floral skirt. Red patches joined the pretty garden of flowers. An eery silence was around us. People stared at this strange vision on the pavement. It couldn't be my brother. It couldn't be.

The police had also arrived.

"I will have to ask you a few questions," the police officer addressed me. He wanted to rule out any foul play. I was interrogated to find out if somebody had pushed him. Eoghan was conscious now.

"I jumped. I jumped. Nobody pushed me. Why am I still alive?" Eoghan stared ahead. "He'll be okay, *Mevrouw*," the paramedic told me.

I looked across at my elder brother's semi-naked body, lying there with an oxygen mask over his mouth and nose and yelled at him angrily.

"Why now?"

I was only four weeks married. Lucas had sorted everything out so beautifully including Eoghan's job, and his flat was nearly ready. He had been wonderful and now my brother was flinging it all back in his face. I felt guilty. I blamed myself. I could never make up to my husband for this but I would try. I was deeply ashamed that

I had brought this upon Lucas and his family. Attempted suicide was not taken lightly in Christian circles either.

Eoghan had dived from our balcony and landed in a shrubbery, which had saved his fall. He had crawled out onto the nearby pavement.

A little girl on the fifth floor had been watching Batman on the television.

"Mama, Batman is flying outside. I've just seen him!" she had called to her mother.

Her mother had looked outside their window and seen my brother flying past. She had been the one who rang the ambulance.

It seemed that the stress of his time in the States had made him psychotic. He claimed that voices had told him to jump. He had a collapsed lung and a broken jaw. It was a miracle that he survived. This was the beginning of a long journey for my brother.

CHAPTER 18

THIRTY-SIX
A KIND OF HAPPINESS

I worked hard at fitting in and making my marriage a peaceful place to be. Lucas liked me earning my own living and I now worked full-time in the publishing house. I was a publisher's assistant and was responsible for academic journals. Everything was in English, so I could speak English all day with my colleagues. I spoke Dutch at home with Lucas and with all our Dutch friends. In the office, I could have a piece of myself for me.

I loved the contact I had with the professors and couldn't quite believe that I had such a great life with a man who loved me. Lucas worked for an international organization and things went from good to better. We moved from our rented apartment to a house in the country in the beautiful village of Kinderdijk, famous for its windmills. The scenery was spectacular with tens of ancient windmills lining a maze of tranquil canals. When I saw the drawings for the house, I was blown away. We were finally getting our white house and life was complete.

We took camping holidays in Italy and France, and went away for weekends to Belgium and Paris. When Lucas became more involved in the local church, I went to please him. I got involved with the local activities. I did bible studies and was confirmed with Lucas in the Protestant Church. Anything that Lucas wanted to do was okay by me. He loved me and I loved him. Our home had Greek statues in the rose garden as a tribute to our undying love. We gave garden parties for our neighbours every summer and I would sing to my guitar while Lucas would share his stories and pour the wine. We were delighted to tell our love story over and over again. We lived the dream.

Our village was very conservative. It had seventeen different Protestant churches and yet only 15,000 inhabitants. Worshippers for each ranged from light Protestant to black-stockinged, modernity-shunning, almost Amish believers. I didn't mind a bit. I had plenty to keep me busy. Lucas looked after everything and I looked after Lucas. Family gatherings were all in Dutch and any feelings of loneliness were pushed aside because I was lucky to have what I had. Lucas prayed at every mealtime that we should be grateful for what we had and I thanked him every day. If I forgot, I was politely reminded. I was so grateful to him. I was lucky to have him in my life.

"Niamh, don't be so negative. You have everything that your heart desires," Lucas scolded me one day. I had being feeling down and slightly homesick. I wanted to stay at home and not visit some of our Dutch friends. He could go on his own. Guilt started nibbling at me every day. I became exhausted.

I cycled around the village on my purple and gold *omafiets*, the old lady's sit-up-and-beg bicycle favoured by the locals, and people stared. My untidy hair blew in every direction. I was the 'foreigner with the weird clothes'.

"It's not Sunday. Why are you wearing a hat?" my neighbour inquired.

"Every day is Sunday for me. I just like wearing my hats," I protested.

She looked at me as if I was mad.

"You are an exotic flower in a desert," the vicar's wife said to me. She was artistic and full of life. It was the nicest thing anyone said to me during those years.

"Niamh, get out while you can," she whispered, taking my hand in hers. I didn't understand what she meant. Or I didn't want to hear.

I knew my outlandish hats and colourful clothes were frowned upon by the stern and bare-faced locals, but that only made me more determined to assert my difference. Being different was a comfort to me despite feeling more and more isolated from the people around me. I tried to belong but never quite succeeded.

Eoghan's constant battle with his illness wasn't easy either.

"Eoghan, will we go out for a walk around the park?" I asked, having spent an hour getting to the house he shared with other mental patients.

"No, I don't feel like it," Eoghan droned, his voice flat and medicated.

I helped him tidy up his room instead and brought him packets of his much loved cigarettes.

"Will you ring me tonight?" he asked. He looked like a lost and lonely little boy.

"Of course I will, I love you," I replied.

I rang him every day to see how he was getting on. I felt powerless and guilty because Lucas had been so good to him. I was caught in a cycle of guilt and appeasing. I hoped Lucas' family didn't think that we were mad.

Guilt and disconnection sapped my creative energies. I hardly sang any more. Apart from at work, I seldom even spoke.

My mother reluctantly overcame her fear of flying and became a frequent visitor to our lovely home, visiting us three times a year for three weeks at a time. She was very proud of my accomplishments. I hadn't let her down. I was married to an educated man who could provide for me. She was happy for me. I was happy for Lucas. Everybody was happy.

"Niamh, don't eat that sandwich now. Let's go to the shopping centre. I want to buy some clothes there," Mammy ordered.

"Yes, Mammy. We'll walk there, I think," I replied.

"It'll be good for you. You have to watch your weight again. Men don't like fat women."

Everybody knew me in the shopping centre. It was the only place to go in the area so I went there often. I stopped to speak to some people from the church and introduced Mammy.

"If I'd known you'd be chatting to everybody else, I wouldn't have come," she blurted out. I couldn't please anybody. Mammy's visits became long and tiresome with her and Lucas fighting for my attention. Everybody wanted a piece of me. But I couldn't take a piece for myself.

When I was thirty-six, I had an incredible urge to have a baby. I pleaded with Lucas.

"But I thought we had agreed that we would remain childless? Our lives are better this way. Look at the freedom we have," Lucas said. We enjoyed our freedom too much, he reminded me. He was right. We could come and go as we pleased. Financially, we had it extremely good. We both worked and had childless friends. Despite his resolve I broached the subject of children more and more. I couldn't get rid of the feelings I had. I waited for Lucas to give his permission.

Eventually, two years later, Lucas was ready to attempt fatherhood and I was over the moon. Ten weeks later, I was pregnant.

I went to the hospital alone to have our first ultrasound scan. Lucas was busy at work and anyway, like he said, it wasn't that important. I lay on the bed in the surgery with clear jelly all over my belly and looked vaguely at a black and white computer monitor.

"You need to wait and see, *Mevrouw*," the young female gynaecologist told me. I was confused. Maybe my Dutch wasn't good enough? Maybe she was talking about the sex of the baby and we'd have to wait and see whether we had a boy or a girl?

That evening Lucas told me that it must have been a misunderstanding. I should have asked her to speak in English to me, given the circumstances.

A few days later I felt unwell at work, so came home and lay on the bed. I saw some spotting on my underpants but didn't think anything of it. Lucas had come home from work and we had eaten.

"I have an awful pain in my stomach." I winced and ran to the toilet.

I was almost fifteen weeks pregnant. The pain doubled me over. I didn't want my baby to be born in a toilet.

"Lucas, hurry!" I screamed.

He raced in after me, quick as a flash, carrying a white bucket. My baby was born into that bucket. He was a tiny human being but stunted in his growth. His little face made him look like a shrimp with great big eyes. I wanted to reach out but he was quickly put into a plastic supermarket bag by Lucas. I saw the last of a potential little finger disappear into the whiteness. I knew it was a boy. I just knew, although it was not clear. I was devastated.

We drove in silence to the hospital. I was still in a lot of pain. The plastic bag was in the boot of the car. I wanted him with me. I knew my baby must have been lonely back there but I said nothing, I was too shocked. Lucas was always calm in crisis situations. He knew what to do.

The doctor asked to take away the foetus for analysis. Lucas agreed and handed over the plastic bag that contained my baby. I never saw him again. Everyone was practical and calm around me. I wanted to scream out: "WHERE IS MY BABY?" but I didn't. Ever the coward, I sat there and cried. Lucas and I were shown into a small room to calm down.

"We wouldn't like you to have an accident on the way home," the gynaecologist said before examining me perfunctorily. "Yes, *Mevrouw*, everything is gone. All is clear. You can go home now."

It turned out that I had a thyroid problem and the baby had not been able to develop properly. My baby's remains were disposed of by the hospital. I didn't get to say goodbye.

I found myself apologizing to Lucas.

"It has made me realize that I am ready to be a father. We can try again for another," Lucas said tearfully but steadily, and we embraced.

I blamed myself. I had killed my own baby. Mother Joseph's voice drummed through my head:

"You are an evil seed and will never grow straight and good."

My baby had rejected my body. I resented Lucas for taking him away so heartlessly. We didn't speak about it. We had to move on. We'd make another baby. Lucas was ready now. I looked at him and willed the old feelings of total love to overtake me, but instead, I felt the beginnings of dislike. I suppressed the feeling and held his hand. Lucas was right. It was time to move on and find out how we could try again.

"We'll get you some medication for your thyroid and try again, okay?" he said and went for a walk round the garden.

The baby had been a boy and his name had been Fionn. Lucas and I never discussed it again. No one acknowledged it was a boy but I knew.

My mother wasn't much more supportive.

"It's probably just as well, it would have been a Mongol anyway," she'd said on the phone. "And I'd ordered a top of the range pram at Brown Thomas too."

"I'm sorry, Mammy," I said.

"Now I'll have to go all the way down there and cancel the order."

"I'm sorry, Mammy. For all the trouble."

Later she told me that the staff had had to give her a cup of tea to calm her down. I forgave her for saying such a horrible thing. It was only said in anger and frustration. I buried myself in consoling everybody else.

The day after the miscarriage, Lucas and I took his nephew and niece to Seaworld. The trip had been organised for weeks and it never dawned on me not to go. I didn't deserve to stay at home and rest. I wasn't ill. I couldn't disappoint the children. I sat in the car bleeding profusely and feeling as if my world had ended. As usual, Lucas took charge. Everything was going according to plan. There was no time to dally. We had a beautiful day.

I got pregnant a few months later. I loved the feeling that was growing inside of me but I was terrified that this baby might not be perfect. I prayed to God to keep him or her safe, but I wasn't hopeful. The Lord didn't have a good track record when it came to listening to me.

The hospital made some serious miscalculations. After seventeen hours in labour they decided it was too late for a caesarean.

I watched the contents of my bowels and everything else spill out onto the square white paper towel. I couldn't push any more. My insides were empty. My baby was stuck in tight and had to be removed from my body with steel forceps. When the cold metal entered my womanhood, I felt violated. I had twenty six stitches and thought I deserved them. The pain was excruciating. I made a pact with the devil: "I will do anything so long as she is healthy. You can take me to your den and I will be your whore and companion."

I was that little girl again in the convent. I begged God and the angels to protect me too, to be on the safe side. As I felt them cutting through my vagina, I saw my carousel horse again, the one from that dark day in the wardrobe. The cold steel of the forceps raped me once again. I begged my carousel horse to go faster and take me away from this dreadful onslaught.

"Be a good girl now," I heard the nurse whisper.

I will be a good girl, I thought. Just give me my baby. Just let her live.

"You are a big girl now," flashed into my mind. Where had I heard those words before? I couldn't remember. It was all hazy. I must have been hallucinating.

Our daughter, Oisin, was born in August 1996 and we were absolutely thrilled. A beautiful, healthy child had been given to me. I didn't deserve her. She looked at me and I cried out in agony. I was afraid that, in making her safe, I may have sold my soul to the devil. I was terrified to touch her. But when she was placed in my arms I felt a surge of love and compassion.

I swore that I would do everything in my power to protect her as long as I lived. A deep strength emerged in me, one that I'd not felt in a long, long time. I cursed both the devil and God and told them to leave us alone. Then I begged them for mercy and for them to allow me to love her and be a good mother. I loved her unconditionally.

"*Mevrouw*, when was the last time you peed?" a nurse inquired.

"I don't remember," I replied looking down at my swollen ankles.

A catheter was roughly inserted into my bruised and bloodied body. I was violated again. I couldn't protest. I held my newborn in my arms and her tiny fingers curled around my index finger. I sang her the songs I had sung throughout my pregnancy. She listened contentedly. My voice had returned.

I lay in the hospital bed and visitors came and went. I hardly noticed them. All I could see was my beautiful baby in her little glass bed beside me.

"*Mevrouw*, we have to take your baby away to intensive care. She has a fever and some other complications," the young blond nurse said, matter of factly.

"She won't die, will she? My baby won't die?" I asked pathetically.

"She's perfectly okay; they just have to take her down to the baby unit. I'll go with them," Lucas calmly explained. He patted my hand and they were gone.

I watched my baby in her glass bed disappear with Lucas and the nurse. Suddenly, I was terrified.

"Mammy, where are you?" I had said on the phone to her.

"I think it's better for me to come over when the baby and you are settled at home," Mammy had replied. She came when Oisin was seven weeks' old. I knew it was hard for her to see her 'baby' with a baby. Her reaction was a huge disappointment to me. Instead of love for her grandchild and me I received disapproval. I felt that I had no-one yet again. My Dutch friends didn't understand my aloneness. They always had their families within reach.

"The Dutch system is great. When you go home, you get a nurse for a week to look after you and the baby. You don't get that in Ireland, do you?" Yes, they were right. I was so bloody lucky as a foreigner to be treated so well. I shouldn't complain. So I didn't.

"I don't deserve this baby. That's why they have taken my baby away from me," was the silent scream that went round and round in my head.

"Here is a breast pump," she said, again matter-of-factly. "We will have to feed her through a tube. You can go down and see her whenever you like. Just make sure that you have enough milk for her." The older nurse spoke to me. I looked at her through my mist of tears.

I was handed a cold inanimate object and given instructions on how to pump milk from my swollen breasts. I felt nothing. My nipples were numb.

The young mother in the next bed to me had had twins. Her babies were beside her and her visitors came and went laden with gifts and greetings. She glowed in her new role. I watched in awe. They had taken my baby away already. That proved I didn't deserve her. I wondered whether I would ever see her again. My neighbour's visitors looked at me with pity and avoided my gaze. I was back at the convent again. My classmates refused to look at me. I heard their whispers echoing in the white ward. I bent my head and wished Mammy was with me.

Eoghan was the only one who took me in his arms and cried with me.

"They are bastards," he said, his swollen face, red with anger and trembling with a combination of medication and frustration. That was my brother's answer to a lot of things.

"Niamh, I love you. The bloody bastards. I'll kill them all. I'll go to Belgium and buy a shotgun and shoot the bastards," he growled.

"Ah, Eoghan now don't be like that. It's not all that bad," I reassured him. But the thought of him killing a few people actually consoled me. I felt like strangling a few people myself. This was the guy they said was delusional, but here was the one person who understood my pain and bewilderment. He held my hand and told me that it would be all right. That was all I wanted to hear. It should have been Lucas taking me in his arms. But he was being practical and down-to-earth as usual.

"Be grateful that we have a healthy baby girl," he said. He was right. I would have to get on with the situation. I was very grateful indeed. His family agreed wholeheartedly.

"God has given you this wonderful gift," his sister said. She proceeded to tell me about the horrific birth of one of her children. We had to grin and bear it. I had no one to turn to. They were right. I was being dramatic and weak. But a part of me hated them all. Their callousness was what I didn't need. I wanted somebody to embrace me and tell me that it would be okay. I hated myself for being needy. They were good people. I was the bad one. They would keep me on the good road. I just needed guidance.

When I became delirious they discovered that I too had an infection with a high fever. Lucas saw more of Oisin than I did. I was weak and disoriented. They wanted me to stop using the breast pump. I refused. I was determined that I would breast-feed my baby. They said that the antibiotics would affect the quality of the milk. I didn't listen.

The matron came by to see how I was doing. Her rounds were timed and I could not take up much of her time.

"I have heard that you are having some difficulty adjusting to motherhood," she said and looked at me, as if expecting me to snap out of it.

"My baby is somewhere else. The pump is so cold. I want my baby back with me," I whimpered to a young nurse who had come along too. I could not talk to a matron who reminded me of Mother Joseph.

They left the room and I thought I had a reprieve. But when they returned she had reinforcements with her. Clearly, she had no idea how to deal with such an emotional outburst and by then I had developed quite a reputation for not wanting anyone to go anywhere near my vagina. They wanted to check that everything was healing okay.

The matron looked pleased with herself. She had a solution. Then I noticed that she had a small mirror in her hand.

"It is my experience that if you look at where your baby came from, you will give it a place in the healing process, both emotionally and physically. We know that you have had a difficult labour but you have to realise that you are not twenty-five any more. Now, be a good woman and have a look at yourself."

She pulled across the white curtain and the metal rings shone in the bright hospital lights. Her taut, agile body moved towards me. She was coming to get me. She was going to hurt me.

I screamed inwardly as I caught a glimpse of my battered womanhood in the mirror. I felt sick and disgusted.

"You see now," she said. "No more tears or protestations. This will help you be a better mother to your baby."

She walked off, glancing at her watch. It had taken exactly ten minutes to push me over a black precipice. I was nine again and curled up in a ball in the bed. The young nurse drew aside the curtain, tucked me into the crisp clean sheets and gave me a sleeping tablet.

"It will make you feel better," she said. "Tomorrow will be a better day for you. Sleep is a great healer."

She looked at me hesitantly. I knew that she knew tomorrow would not heal my wounds. She avoided my glassy gaze and strolled out of the room. I was alone again.

Lucas came to visit me later. We talked excitedly about our new baby. When he left, I lay back, exhausted. I could relax again. Acting the role of happy mother was very tiring. I wanted to die. My baby wouldn't miss me. She didn't even know me.

Ten days later, I put her on my breast for the first time. The nurses didn't have much hope that she would take to my breast.

"Don't pay any attention to them," a male nurse called Bram whispered gently in my ear. "If you really want it to, it will happen."

Oisin and I looked at each other.

"Okay kiddo, it's now or never," I said to her. "Let's do this together."

And we did. She took to my breast and I looked down in awe. These were the breasts that had been battered and bruised. These were the breasts that had been punched and pinched. These were the breasts that had been bitten and lusted after. These were the breasts that had been flattened and hidden for many years. These were the breasts that had been spat on.

Yet these breasts were now giving life to my child. I looked down at her little head bobbing as she sucked greedily and I felt an overwhelming joy. The tears rolled down my cheeks and I felt something that I had not felt for such a long, long time: a feeling of having accomplished something great.

"Does it hurt? If it's too painful, you can stop," the nurse said.

I shook my head. I didn't reply. In the end I breast-fed for nearly a year. It was the most wonderful and amazing experience of my life and Oisin thrived. There was no better gift that I could have been given. I thanked God for giving me this opportunity. I thanked the devil for not having taken her away from me. I warned both of them to keep their distance. I was a lioness protecting her young. I had great difficulty letting somebody else hold her.

CHAPTER 19

FORTY
DIFFERENT

Oisin was everything to me but my fears still haunted me. There were potential threats in every corner. I checked in on her many times a night. Broken sleep and the threat of danger took their toll, but I pushed myself forward to be the perfect wife and mother. I had to prove to the world that I was not just a good mother, but an excellent one.

It was decided that I should be a stay-at-home mother. It would be better for Oisin and I agreed. I could not bear the idea of Oisin being taken to child-care every morning and being brought up by a stranger. We were lucky that we could afford for Lucas to be the sole bread winner.

I walked into my office when Oisin was three months old and handed in my notice. I was relieved. I didn't have to work on computers and appease nutty academics anymore. My new life would be wonderful with my baby and loving husband.

I could see windmills from my bedroom window. They were lined up neatly in a row and I counted them one by one with my finger on the newly-washed windows. Lucas's married sister, Hannah, had done a good job in washing them. They gleamed. It gave me a certain satisfaction to put my fingerprint on the perfect glass and press lightly so that a row of dots spoiled the perfect scene. Hannah had offered to help me clean the house.

She was an expert in cleaning. I watched her as she dusted and vacuumed. I pretended to be interested in her feats but screamed 'Bored!' in my mind.

"Look, Niamh, this is how you use the squeegee and the cloth. It's very easy really," she continued. All I wanted to do was run away as quickly as possible with Oisin to the nearest playground or cycle over the endless paths in the marshy *polder* beneath an open sky.

We could skate on the local lake in the winter. I felt imprisoned in the chocolate box painting. I couldn't get out. I cycled with Oisin on the little seat in front of me and stopped to take photos of the wonderful scenery that surrounded us. I saw Japanese tourists reacting to the incredible view and felt guilty that I took it for granted.

"We have to be grateful for what God has given us and pray in gratitude every day," Lucas reminded me at the kitchen table, whilst reading a passage from the bible.

I stared ahead and didn't sing psalms in my confused brain but rebellious verses:

"I'm bored out of my head.
Let me go to bed."

My neighbours were all stay-at-home mums too. They had loads of children; I had one. They were extremely churchy and I had nothing in common with them. On Mondays they would all go out onto the street and sweep the step and path outside their homes. Tuesdays was washing the windows day. I peeped out and dreaded seeing them looking in at me looking out! Oisin and I would wave at them from the window and I would get out all her toys and we would create our own world on the sitting room floor. I bought extravagant presents for her and the whole house was littered with toys. I played with them more often than she did. She preferred the boxes that they came in. Lucas gave me money to buy the groceries and I blew it all on a giant swimming pool for the garden. Oisin and I played for hours in the water until Lucas came home. I hurriedly went to make the dinner with what was left in the fridge.

"Daddy's home! Dinner will be ready in a moment," I panted, smiling placatingly at my husband.

"That's okay," Lucas said. I never knew then if he was angry or just indifferent. I didn't know what to think. But it was a happy household in general. Our priorities were just different. Oisin could run around barefoot and scream with all her might. I saw her as a very sociable, loving human being.

"She's very busy, isn't she? Does she ever take a nap? Would you not put her in her playpen?" a neighbour inquired.

"Playpens are prisons and stop children from exploring their environment. She's not a dog," I retaliated.

I would never stop Oisin from being who she wants to be. I was determined about that. Perhaps I went overboard in my enthusiasm, but it was better than creating a robot without a heart, just like me. She ran wildly through the house and her friends followed her.

"Niamh, could you look after Jantine, Ellen, Joop, Cees, Josephine en Manuel for a few hours while I go shopping?"

"No problem, take your time," I replied. I was very popular for childminding. I never refused. Our house was an open invitation to mayhem. The children would go home to their squeaky clean homes and leave behind a trail of destruction. I did my best to clean the mess up before Lucas came home. I didn't always succeed. His irritation fed my rebelliousness.

"You don't have to spend three days to prepare a Halloween party for the kids," Lucas looked at me inquiringly. He looked around at the home-made cave in the living-room, the dungeon in the kitchen, as he was struggling through the fake spider cobwebs to get to the hallway. He tripped into a ghostly apparition hanging from the ceiling. It let out an almighty "oooooooooooooooooooooooooh," and I laughed.

"I'm sorry, Lucas. Maybe I went a bit overboard," I wanted to say, but I didn't. I was tired of apologizing.

Lucas expected me to do my best as the perfect homemaker and mother. His mother and his sisters were expert in that field. His background was rural and practical. I had been brought up with the city and confusion. Mammy loved beautiful things but her skills as a good housekeeper were not optimal. She just did what had to be done. The immaculate appearance of her children was the most important factor in her life. I know it was perfectly reasonable to expect it of me. He found the idea of paying for somebody to come in to clean once a week quite ludicrous. Hannah had already helped out more than enough. It was my job to take on these chores.

"I am so busy with Oisin. Can't Hannah stay for a little while?" I pleaded.

"Niamh, it's time to do your duty. You are now a full-time mother and all the other women seem to know how to do it. It's a question of doing. I'm tired of your negative excuses."

He was right. I was a stupid, sloppy housewife. I had to do better. I had to please the whole world and fit in with the stay-at-home work force in this perfect little community.

I tried to turn myself into a responsible mother and wife. God knows, I tried, but more often than not, I would run off with the pram and walk for hours until it was time to go home to make dinner. I felt the other mothers were laughing at me.

"Shall we start a book club?" I suggested one day while sharing see-through cups of black tea with them after bible study.

"Will it be a Christian book club?" they asked.

My mouth dropped open.

"My husband won't allow me read other kinds of books," skinny Gerda said shyly.

"We can read anything you like, so long as we read something," I replied impatiently. But I knew it would not happen. Perish the thought of anything different taking place here.

I felt I had landed in a Stepford wives movie. Everybody did their chores and stayed at home. I, on the other hand would run as fast as I could to get away from the prying eyes of the village. Lucas loved living here. He had found a place that felt like home. My feelings of isolation, although familiar, didn't help the situation.

Oisin was growing fast and we would spend hours in the local playground.

I would push her on the swing, back and forth endlessly. She loved it. I adored watching her reach up to touch the blue sky, her flaxen hair blowing in the wind. I wanted her to have the freedom that I never had. She would scream out with sheer pleasure when I pushed her higher and higher. I would bring our lunch with us and a big plaid blanket would cover the cold concrete playground. Her first word was 'picnic'. As our daughter grew, I made sure that she would never suffer creatively. I sang songs to her and she listened. She had a remarkable ear for music and imitated flawlessly.

I took her to 'music on the lap' classes. This was a class for two-year-olds and the whole class of mothers and kids sang "The Wheels on the Bus go Round and Round" and other songs in Dutch. I didn't want Oisin to have difficulties with Dutch. But I spoke only English to her. I wanted her to be totally bilingual. I sang a little bit too passionately sometimes and the other mothers would look at me. I forgot that I was the mother not the child.

The music teacher had a bear puppet:

"What is your name," the bear asked.

"I am Niamh," I replied

There was an embarrassed silence.

"I meant the children to answer," the small stern-faced teacher looked at me. Some mothers giggled and I turned away. Oisin looked at me and patted my hand.

"Sorry, Mama", she whispered.

I knew that I would never let her do that again. She would never have to say sorry to me again. I would never let my own child feel sorry for me. It pierced my heart. I would break this stupid pattern if it took the last breath away from me. The only problem was how?

"Mama, violin," Oisin pointed at the beautiful instrument in the music shop window.

She started violin lessons at four years of age and excelled in it. She was playing pieces from Bach at five. Her lessons were three to four times a week.

From swimming and violin lessons to sport and theatre classes, Oisin excelled in them all. I had no driving licence because I had failed five times. I couldn't concentrate. In Ireland I had driven for ten years but only had a provisional licence. A big L plate was on my car for years. I was terrified to take the test in Holland too. It cost a lot of money.

"Maybe you should get a scooter?" Lucas suggested. I had to cycle and take the bus everywhere. Looking after Oisin was a great distraction from what was really going on. I did my best to be a good housewife and loving mother, in fact, a Stepford wife, myself. I was sure I loved Lucas unconditionally and did everything he asked me to. Indeed, I loved him more than I loved myself, though maybe that wasn't so difficult. I was determined that everybody would be happy. It never crossed my mind that I deserved to be happy too. Lucas was very kind to me after all. He loved me. He loved me.

While I ran in one direction while he was out at work, Lucas started running the moment he came home. He became very slim and fit, while I, on the other hand started putting on weight. When we met he was a plump little man. Now, when we stood side by side, he seemed taller than me. I, on the other hand looked smaller and plumper. I was happy that he was getting his life in order. I wanted him to be a success. It never dawned on me that I could be as well. I overate and my underactive thyroid didn't help. But it didn't matter. Everybody was happy around me and that's all that mattered. My layer of fat was comforting and safe. Nobody could get through to me now. Cadbury's chocolate was my friend. He came out of my drawer in the evening and we chomped happily together on the bright yellow settee. Sometimes, I would hide his wrappings when Lucas came home. After a while, I stopped. Coloured foil and papers littered the coffee table and Lucas said nothing. He loved me for who I was. I appreciated that. He was a good husband and father.

When Oisin was five months old we decided to try for another baby, but my age was against me. Lucas and I had a deal.

"Niamh, we discussed this. The deal is to have five treatments to give us the best shot," he stated efficiently.

"Can we just see what happens after the first few treatments?"

"Niamh, now come on now. Don't be so negative, always negative. It will be okay." He walked away.

I felt guilt yet again for not being more enthusiastic but a part of me felt I couldn't cope with another baby. Oisin hardly slept and being a stay-at-home Mom was not easy.

"These injections encourage your ovulation and you will have an increased chance of conceiving because of your age," Dr Piper explained.

I had to inject myself. The young nurse showed me how but I couldn't do it. Another disappointment! Lucas would have to drive me for the injections to the hospital or I would take the bus. Lucas really wanted another child. I convinced myself that I did too. Two beautiful children in a beautiful house with a beautiful view of the Kinderdijk windmills outside our bedroom window.

I lived from month to month with disappointment. Lovemaking was robotic and focused only on our goal. I was numb to my grief and guilt. My body weight ballooned. I felt as bloated as an inflatable Michelin man. My mood swings didn't help and at times I could hardly function. I battled on for Oisin's sake.

One rainy November, just before my forty-second birthday, I paid another trip to the gynaecologist. Lucas accompanied me on these appointments. He needed to ensure I got my facts right.

"Niamh, you have a healthy child. Cut your losses and move on. Your body cannot take any more," he said.

Lucas leaned over to me and gave me a look that gently reminded me that we had had a deal.

"Niamh, the deal was five treatments. It would be such a pity to stop now. I think the next one could take and you would be very disappointed if you stopped now," Lucas said.

"But I can't cope. Please let me stop. Please?" I pleaded.

"Don't be so negative. It's just one more," he said coldly.

He had not heard a word I said. I would have to endure one more hormone treatment. A deal was a deal. I acquiesced. I couldn't disappoint him any more than I had already. I felt needy and negative. He was right. I just had to bite the bullet and get through this. Lucas was my life and he knew best. He always knew best. Resentment began to seep in but I suppressed it, squashing it as flat as my pre-teen breasts beneath layers of vests. I made it go away and tried to focus on what I was supposed to do. Make him another baby.

CHAPTER 20

FORTY-ONE
MAMMY

The telephone rang. I thought it was my mother. She was due to fly over for Oisin's second birthday the following month.

She had just been over to Scotland to see Turlough before he went offshore again. She was not feeling well and had a stomach upset.

The telephone rang.

"Niamh, you need to come home," pleaded Ena, Mammy's good friend. "Your mother is going into hospital for tests."

"What?" I began but Ena had already passed the phone over to Mammy.

"Ach, there's nothing to worry about, Niamh," said Mammy but alarm bells went off in my head. I asked Lucas to take some time off work to look after Oisin and caught the next available flight with Eoghan. Turlough was offshore and was informed. He was arranging a replacement so that he could be flown off the oil-rig. The flight to Dublin was a nightmare. Eoghan was so nervous and I couldn't think straight.

"When can I have a cigarette? I'm going mad here," Eoghan gritting his teeth

"We'll be touching down any minute now, hold on," I replied.

He repeated his question every ten minutes and I had to keep on reassuring him. I felt like hammering him over the head but knew he couldn't help it. My own head was a confused mist of questions and fears.

At the hospital, my mother looked calm if a little pale. I walked up to her bed and sat on the pale blue counterpane.

"You look well," she said. "But you have put on weight, now, haven't you?"

I took her dainty hand and tried not to cry. She hated fuss.

"You look well yourself." Mammy's face looked tanned and healthy.

Mammy had cancer of the liver. She became increasingly jaundiced as the days went by. Her now grey blonde hair was looking the worse for wear but she didn't look her sixty-nine years. Her face was still unwrinkled and smooth.

"Mammy, I'm getting the hairdresser to come and do your hair for you. You always feel better when it's done," I said chirpily.

She did. She sat up in her bed, looking the lady that she was.

I massaged her feet daily and we shared intimate moments. We recounted events from my childhood and she spoke about my father. She had not spoken about him for years. I looked at this petite woman sitting up in the bed and realised how much I loved her. She had battled many things in her own life. She had been left to fend for three young children at an early age and had spent more than half of her married life on her own. She had never really spoken about her own youth.

"Niamh, would you go and buy me a nice lacy nightdress from Marks and Spencer?" she asked.

I bought her a lovely pink one with pink rosebuds. She asked me to help her put it on.

"Mammy, you look gorgeous!" I said. I meant it. Her hollow cheeks were orangey-yellow in the hospital light and her bright blue eyes twinkled at me.

"Mammy, you're coming home tomorrow," I said. "I won't be along tonight as I'll be getting your room ready."

"Grand, grand," she said, before adding with a smile, "Niamh, I have to say you've got a lot more organised."

I waved goodbye and that was the last time I saw her alive.

I was glad that Eoghan had his special moments with her also. They'd always had a love-hate relationship and they could reconcile their differences. Turlough also had quality time with her too. She waited for him to come. She saw all her three children before she died.

My brothers and my sister-in-law, Emer, and I were all staying over at Mammy's house. The phone rang at around eleven that night and we all rushed to the hospital. Mammy had died ten minutes earlier, in her sleep in her new pink lace nightie.

"Now, I'm just going for a nice little sleep," she had told the nurse. The nurse turned around but she was gone.

We had all been too late. She was still warm and I took her little hand and slipped her wedding ring onto my finger. The nurse told us that she had never asked for anything. She was the model patient. They were surprised at how quickly it had all happened.

"She chose her own time to die," the nurse said.

She had died four days before Oisin turned two.

I looked down at her dead body. This was the woman who had waited all her life for something to happen - the woman who had waited for her husband to come home. This was the woman who decided to die in the hospital rather than wait for death at home. She had had enough of waiting.

I stood up and recited in the hospital ward: "Although I walk through the valley of death, I fear no evil." My words echoed through the cold, sterile ward and I heard my brothers sobbing. It was time to say goodbye.

She came home the next day and we laid her out in her bedroom. Her face was peaceful but her skin had turned green. I began to feel frightened and hated myself for feeling that way. The cancer was still rotting away at her, even in death. I screamed at it and cursed it for taking her. I felt her soft curls in my hands and remembered how she loved to go to the hairdresser for her weekly wash-and-set.

"Mammy, Mammy, come back to me. I am a big girl now. I will look after you."

My tears fell on the flowery bedspread and a wet patch formed near her folded hands. I was afraid to touch them. I could not bear to feel the coldness that had enveloped her body.

I cried for all the things we had not said to each other. I cried for all the countless arguments and stupid misunderstandings. I cried for her never reaching her full potential. I cried for having disappointed her. I cried for her last moments alone. I cried for never having told her my darkest secrets.

I blew her a last kiss and went out into the sunshine. She was cremated. She hated graveyards and when I was a very young girl riding in the bus with her, she had said: "Niamh, never let them bury me in the cold, dark earth."

My brothers and I were distraught. She had been our guiding light throughout our lives. She protected and loved us despite her little eccentricities. I felt like a real orphan now. I had to go back to another country and leave all the memories behind. I had to grieve in another country.

The call of the cold blade of the knife became very strong. The only thing that stopped me from joining my mother was Oisin. I couldn't discuss my grief with anyone. When I rang Lucas back at home, he flew over for the funeral and brought Oisin with him. As it turned out, he stayed at the house and looked after Oisin while my family went to the funeral.

"Children don't belong at funerals," my mother had always said.

We did, however, circle the area with the black hearse to honour the house where Mammy lived. Lucas and Oisin waved to us from the house; the house where I grew up and the house where Mammy would never stand again at the front door. I felt more disconnected than ever from my husband. He should have been by my side and yet I didn't want him there. Somebody had to look after Oisin after all. Two days after the funeral, we flew home to the Netherlands. Lucas thought it best that we get on with our lives as quickly as possible. Eoghan was drinking too much and we had to get him back to his 'protected living'. Nobody thought that I might want to stay.

I looked out the aeroplane window. I saw the patches of green that were Ireland getting smaller and smaller and had an overwhelming feeling of loss and displacement. My mother's urn was tucked between my legs. I thought of Mother Joseph bashing my beret and my mother fixing it again. Mammy was coming back to Holland with me. Mammy's ashes were coming home with me.

I organised Oisin's second birthday party a few days after returning. It was a great party. Colourful balloons swung from the ceilings in the house and two tables full of food greeted the guests. The trees outside were decorated with Chinese lanterns and they swayed in the wind. Bright red and blue tents scattered the lawn. I heard squeals of delight as the toddlers zipped and unzipped themselves from their new make-believe homes. Oisin's screams echoed over the other children's.

"Circus, circus," she screamed. The other children joined in and I saw some raised eyebrows from the more reserved parents.

"Ssh, calm down now," or "You'll be sick with all those sweets". I had lollies hanging from the rose bushes and a small tunnel, which the children had to crawl through. It was filled with small boxes of brightly coloured sweets. I wanted a paradise for these young children. Lots of parents and family were seated in the rose garden, gazing at the excess. I felt their discomfort. A lot of these friends were churchgoers and lived frugal lives. It was too over-the-top for them. All I wanted was to make everybody happy. Could they not see that? Lucas's family sat all together and I felt even more of an outsider looking in. Oisin's birthday cake was a giant Winnie the

Pooh, her favourite character. People felt awkward. They avoided eye contact and mumbled their condolences. It was about the children today. It was Oisin's birthday. It was a time for celebration. Time to move on. Lucas was right. It was a beautiful sunny day. We could eat outside in the sunshine. Lucas was happy toasting our daughter. Who was I to spoil the wonderful celebration?

I went upstairs to our bedroom and took out Mammy's urn and told her about the party. I sat on the double bed and hugged the cold urn to my body. I heard children screaming and babies crying. I heard laughter and murmured conversations downstairs. The sun spilled through the bedroom and I sat there singing my Mammy's favourite song, *Somewhere Over the Rainbow*.

I put the urn back into my favourite oriental cupboard. Mammy had loved the painted bluebirds on the black lacquered doors. I blew a kiss into the shadows. I went downstairs and laughed like the rest of them. Oisin was blowing bubbles. I caught one and burst it. It splashed in my face and I closed my eyes. I didn't want to be there. But where did I want to be?

The garden fountain spewed out water from one large concrete basin into the smaller one underneath it. I found myself wishing that I were the droplets of water that escaped from the fountain. They landed on the newly-laid green lawn. They at least could run into the shadows of the rose bush. I had to sit amongst all these strangers. A mother approached holding a glass of white wine.

"Niamh, a great party as always," she said. "Sorry to hear about your mother."

No, you're not, I thought. You just had to say that out of politeness. My mother is upstairs locked away in a cupboard. Would you like to see her? You stupid, stupid bitch, I thought. It was as if my suppressed emotion was having difficulty staying submerged. It threatened, like the fountain, to spill over.

"Thanks, and yeah, it was very sad," I heard myself saying.

Lucas approached and I wanted him to throw his arms around me and tell me that it would be okay. He didn't. Oisin's little footsteps approached. She put out her arms to me and I held her as if I would never let her go. She wriggled and ran away. Her pale blond curls blew in the light breeze. I ate another piece of birthday cake and felt sick inside.

I moved towards the crowd, held my head high and the Red Sea parted. I made a joke and everybody laughed. All eyes were on me and I played the part of a very good hostess. Hell, I was a damned good hostess.

I still hadn't fallen pregnant and it was time to take action.

"Lucas, I can't go on like this, thinking every month will be better. I need closure now. Would you consider a vasectomy?" I pleaded.

"I read on the net that a man has a one per cent chance of getting prostate cancer if he has that procedure. I would have to really consider it," Lucas replied businesslike as ever.

I wanted him to say that he would do anything for me. After all, I had given birth and gone through all the horrific hormone treatments. But I knew that his head always ruled his heart. I expected that response. I was tired of waiting. I was stuck in no man's land. In the end I booked myself in for the operation without telling him until the last minute. I had to get this sorted once and for all. Though little more than a baby, herself, Oisin needed me more than ever. I wanted to see her growing up. I told Lucas the day before I went in for the operation.

"If that's what you want to do," he said calmly.

I wanted him to say that he would do something for me. But, I didn't blame him really. He wasn't capable of seeing my pain, anger and frustration. I didn't know the man standing in front of me. Maybe, I never did. We lived parallel lives in a parallel universe. His world was one of logic and rationalization. Mine, of emotion and confusion. I had never felt so lonely in all my life.

"There is nothing worse than feeling lonely in a relationship. I would prefer to be lonely on my own," a recently divorced girlfriend had said to me. These words echoed in my mind.

I woke up from the anaesthetic and cried. I cried and cried. I cried over the death of my mother. I cried over having failed again. I couldn't give my husband what he wanted. Oisin was two and a half and sat on the hospital bed playing with her dolly. I had to go on for her. The thought didn't enter my head that I should be going on for *me*.

Lucas stood beside my hospital bed once I had come round and took my hand. I grasped it. I couldn't live without him. He was my saviour. I wept tears of confusion and hurt. There was no alternative. I was linked to him financially and emotionally. He told me what to do. He gave me money when necessary. He controlled my life, my every move. I thought that was what love was all about.

When Oisin was at school, I tried to do things around the house. I did my best to achieve normality. Holidays were always active and adventurous. I dreaded them. I can honestly say that I visited Italy, France and Spain but all the camp sites looked the same. It was great for a young child and Lucas loved it. I just wanted to sleep and recover from the struggles of being the good wife and mother. I hated the 'toilet roll' under my arm scene, going to the communal toilets. I didn't want to sound ungrateful. Lucas provided a good home for us. I was not working. He was the sole breadwinner. I had to respect that.

And life went on. I was so caught up in Oisin's life that I hardly paid attention to my own emptiness. But as she got older, I realised that I could not and would not live her life for her. I was determined not to be her captor as my mother had been mine. I gave her lots of freedom to develop. I invested all my time into making sure that she would be a happy and developed child. Lucas had his freedom too. I encouraged him in whatever he wanted to do.

"Niamh, I'm going to the sauna tonight with the lads."

"No problem," I said. I was glad to have some time to myself as well. I just wanted Lucas to be happy. My weight gain had resulted in me snoring dreadfully.

"Niamh, I can't sleep with you. The noise is too much," Lucas stated.

I understood. Lucas was a light sleeper and I kept him awake. He had to be fit for his work. We started sleeping separately. I was devastated. No intimate moments. It was never about the sex with me. It was about the chats and closeness in the dark of the night. I cried myself to sleep but out of pride, pretended that it didn't affect me. Lucas went up to the attic and I went to the bedroom. The gap became greater over the years. I longed for some sort of closeness again but didn't reach out. I was afraid of being rejected.

We moved to another house to be nearer The Hague because I was very unhappy living in the country. I begged Lucas to consider moving because I was becoming crazy in such a conservative village. He had also just changed jobs and it would be easier to move nearer The Hague. I didn't realize that the move affected Lucas so much. I had taken him away from his life in the village and his friends from the church. Was I being selfish? That move was the beginning of the end of our relationship. We moved to Rijswijk, a small town outside the Hague. Oisin was six years old. Another place, but the same old me.

I launched myself fully into being the perfect mother. I created wonderful themed birthday parties. Outlandish Halloween parties for the children in the area. I organized walks in the dark with cut-out pumpkins and trick-or-treats for the local children.

"Mammy, I would love a 'Finding Nemo' party," Oisin begged.

"Your wish is my every command," I replied, as she ran to play outside.

I spent days cutting out tropical fishes, hanging them from the ceiling. The whole living room looked like a giant aquarium. Twenty six children came running in to celebrate Oisin's eighth birthday. An explosion of colour greeted them. It was magical. There was a Pocahontas party, with everybody dressed up as squaws and Indians, howling through the house. Nothing was too much for me. I had to give her the best childhood possible. Lucas looked on and hardly said anything at this stage. I had children in to bake special little cakes to take home. Sprinkles of silver and chocolate littered the floor. I hardly had the energy to tidy up. I became a member on the Parents' Committee at school. I was there to help with all the school events from Easter to Christmas, and the special sports days. I was running on empty. Oisin was up early in the morning to practice her violin. I sat with her and read her music with her. I encouraged her in every possible way. She had joined the local softball team. I took her to practice and collected her.

"Mammy, can Ellen, Priscilla, Fons and Stewart come over and play after school?"

"Of course, sweetheart, everybody is welcome," I smiled.

For my fiftieth birthday, Lucas booked a holiday to Africa. Oisin was so excited about it. She was eleven years old. A safari trip was one of her ultimate dreams. Another couple had invited themselves with their three daughters. At the back of my mind I was disappointed that Lucas did not say that he would prefer just the three of us to go. I had thought that this was the perfect time for us to get back on track as a couple. It was an organized trip with adults and their children, anyway so it was better for Oisin to have lots of children to play with.

"Thank you Lucas for this surprise. I am very grateful," I said enthusiastically. I meant it. It was a very expensive trip.

The smells of Africa hit me like a freight train. The colours and vibrancy of the people energized me. I hadn't felt like that for a long, long time. We were collected at Nairobi in a huge safari bus. This would be our home for the next two weeks, travelling around. We had two cooks on board and it was going to be a fantastic adventure. And it was. I loved every minute of it and drank in the sounds of the hyenas, laughing like children in the night. We saw amazing animals on our safari trips and Lucas' constant companion was his camera. The other couples seemed very close and when dinner time came sat in their own little groups, at the large wooden table. I noticed that Oisin sat with a different family every night and Lucas and I hardly ever sat together. It was as if we had totally grown apart. I envied the attractive Hans putting his arm around his beautiful wife, with his small gestures and intimate moments, even among so many people.

One day we visited a Masai village and I saw solidarity among the men and women. The men and women had their own roles to play but yet played an integral part in each other's lives. I entered one of their very small huts.

"Big Mama, you not fit in here. You take up much space," said one of the Masai warriors to me.

I laughed and had a quick look around. I saw a huge bed made from goatskin in the corner. These natives even slept together in such a small area. They could cuddle up to each other and keep each other warm. I longed to have that feeling again and for a moment, wanted to lie down on the rickety construction. Lucas came in. Oisin followed. Two Masai warriors tried to sell us some bracelets. They were beautifully beaded with bright colours.

"You like, you buy," the older one said.

"We don't want, no, we won't buy," said Lucas sternly.

I tried to protest but Lucas became angrier. I had no money with me. Oisin started to cry. It was always the same. We walked out into the sunshine. I felt even more depressed.

The Masai sang a beautiful song for us to welcome us. The rhythms touched my heart. I, in turn sang an Irish tune for them. There was silence. They had never been sung to by the tourists before. I was quickly surrounded by beautiful Masai women who approached me smiling broadly and touching me gently with long, dark fingers. I was honoured to be there. I wanted to stay. We started heading back to camp and two Masai warriors came with us to protect us on our journey back. One warrior held back and I approached him. It was that chance meeting that started the ball moving in my life.

Africa changed my life forever. I knew that I couldn't stay but didn't know how to go. I loved Lucas so much but it was killing me. I thought things would get better. We argued about everything. I rebelled at anything he suggested. I didn't want to be dictated to any more. It was time to grow up. Divorce became inevitable.

CHAPTER 21

FIFTY-TWO
A NEW ME

Note: *To honour this Shamanic workshop, I don't go into great details of the hows and wherefores. Suffice to say that it was a powerful and pure experience, shared by me and the other participants that weekend. It stays sacred. I remain grateful to Thomas and Emer for their role in the events that took place. I would also like to acknowledge Eileen, Thomas' partner, for her support. Her yoga classes were wonderful. The cooks, Catherine and Ester who fed us beautiful food to nourish our physical needs.*

My power animal is only known to me and comes to me in dream time. My spirit guide is a personal guide who appears to me regularly with messages to help me on my path.

Turlough and his wife, Emer, had supported me throughout the divorce and two years on, I was coping admirably, but I was still struggling with my deep secrets.

Emer, who had taken the shamanic path earlier, mentioned an upcoming Shamanic workshop in Aberdeen, Scotland, where they were living. It would be held by renowned shaman, Thomas Grufferty, and Emer herself.

"If it's for you, you will come," Emer said. That was the shamanic philosophy. "I'll pay for the workshop if you get your arse over here," continued Turlough.

An envelope came in the post. I opened it and an orange form slipped out onto the kitchen table. I read the words 'release the past' and 'not for the faint-hearted'. The form was only a formality. Turlough had already paid for the workshop. I felt an incredible urge to sign on a dotted line, but that had been done for me. I knew I was about to be committed not only to the shamanic team but also to myself.

I grabbed the nearest pen. It was green and almost empty. Typically, Oisin had left all her half-chewed pens on the table. I signed on the dotted line all the same. I signed for my new journey. I booked my flight to Aberdeen.

Oisin was staying with Lucas that weekend.

"Mammy, get out of it what you want to put into it," she said to me on her way out the door.

I grinned at her. She was repeating my own advice to her. She grabbed me and embraced me briefly.

I watched her disappearing down the road with her father and Mozart, the dog. Mozart looked back, his brown eyes confused. He hesitated. Should he stay or go? I told him to go. Mozart was my little black-and-white mongrel, who we had saved from certain death. I had seen him in a dirty cage at the back of a pet shop. Mozart was the little dog who accompanied me everywhere. Mozart was my little confidant who listened and whimpered with me. Mozart, who opened doors for me along the way. People loved him and would stop to talk with me. I met many new friends through his sparkly presence. Mozart, my little friend. He trotted after Oisin, and I closed the front door. A white feather blew into the hallway.

I was alone.

The airport was buzzing. At customs, I had to remove my lilac ankle boots, purple trilby hat and my never-ending chains and over-the-top chunky jewellery, while everybody stood back and waited. I prayed that the machine would not go off. I had, after all, deposited almost half my wardrobe into the plastic trays provided.

I sat on the plane and tried not to think. I hummed a tune. It was a tune of long ago, from a time that I had forgotten. A time that I did not want to remember. Where was this coming from? Little did I know that my healing had already begun.

"Scrunch goes the crunch of my new shoes."

Thomas looked at me with his piercing blue eyes. He was a surprisingly young man. He took my hand.

"I was expecting an old man with a long white beard," I laughed nervously.

Judging from his reaction, I wasn't the first person to say that to him.

"Niamh, you got tired of waiting," he said to me.

He looked at me with such intensity. I knew then that he could see through to my soul. I wanted to run. The workshop was held outside Aberdeen, in a beautiful country setting. I saw a lake in the distance.

The other participants arrived and dispersed to their rooms to unpack. Emer came with me. This time, I put my clothes in the wardrobe with confidence. There was nowhere to run any more. I was here. I was going to see this through to the very end. I walked over to the window and spotted the lake in the distance. Maybe I could escape to there? Could I swim to the little island?

"You might as well stay, now that you're here, kiddo," Emer said and took my hand. Her slender fingers entwined with mine. I always loved my sister-in-law and felt even more love for her at that moment. I was sharing a room with her and Turlough. He looked at me encouragingly. He had been on many of these Shamanic weekends. This weekend, however was even more significant for him. He had picked up a virus in Dubai and it had attacked his heart. He stood there, pale and sweaty but convinced that everything would be okay. I was very concerned for him. I knew later that I didn't have to be. It was as if his heart had 'kick-started' the whole weekend for me.

The 'healing' room was actually just a room in the lodge in which we were staying. It was plain, although mats and blankets were scattered over the floor. Thomas and Emer stood there waiting for us. The curtained windows were drawn, which gave it a warm, cosy feeling.

When I entered this room I had an overwhelming feeling of safety. A feeling that I had never experienced this strongly, not even as a child. I wanted to drink in its pureness and goodness.

"I never want to leave this room," I said to another participant. She felt the same. I lay down on my side and curled up in a ball. Every person in that room was on their own journey. Nobody judged or ridiculed. We were all there for a purpose. I knew instinctively that this weekend would change my life. I saw Thomas and Emer standing there, powerful and pure. I thought I saw a blinding white light surrounding them.

We completed many meditation exercises that weekend. The most fascinating for me was the one in which we had to hunt down our fears and pain. I thought I was coming to purge myself of a failed marriage. The gods had other things in mind for me. I was ready to face whatever was thrown at me.

"Niamh, I'm ready," I said to myself, remaining remarkably calm. My eyes were closed and I held on to my rubber mat for support. I had to make this journey.

I went down a tunnel and there I confronted my life. I saw my pearly white shoes, and my flaxen curls being pulled. I felt my bruised cheek and pained knuckles. The nuns waved and smiled at me.

"I forgive you. You didn't understand me," I called out to them.

I saw myself looking at myself as a young child. I didn't want to go there. I heard a voice in the tunnel with me.

"Niamh, I won't leave you behind. You have to go on." It was Thomas.

I saw my first communion and the brown confessional box. I went further down the tunnel. My white lace dress flew ahead of me. I ran to catch it. I saw the dark oak wardrobe and I opened it. I stared at the little white-haired girl tossing her pink rosebud underpants into the darkness. She looked at me and I cried with her. I reached out to embrace her and she held me warmly and tightly and encouraged me to go on to the next part of my journey.

I took a spear and thrust it into Mr Hawthorn's groin. I told him that it was never my fault. I saw him fading away and I forgave him.

"They are only words Niamh," Ronka said to me. "They are not you." She held my hand and we went together to my confirmation. We went through all the major events in my life.

"Hello." It was Daddy speaking to me and suddenly I didn't want to continue.

I saw the teenager on the pier and the swelling sea almost engulfing her.

"Daddy, I'm sorry; forgive me," I pleaded.

I saw his body at the bottom of the South China Sea. He smiled at me to go on.

"I'm always with you, Niamh," he said. "Forgive yourself, forgive yourself."

We stopped at the beach in Greece. I screamed to stop now.

"No, please don't let me go there."

"I won't leave you behind," Thomas's voice repeated through the darkness. I trusted him. I had to go on. I knew Emer was encouraging me. Her presence was evident throughout the experience.

I saw my bruised body in the darkness and the white camisole top that Mammy had bought for me. Its white buttons gleamed at me. The three men walked away into the shadows.

"It wasn't your fault. It never was your fault," little Niamh said to me. I screamed at the men and threw three spears in their direction. They tumbled like bowling balls and I shouted obscenities at them.

"You bastards, it was never my fault. You bloody bastards, you nearly killed me."

I forgave them because I had to move on. I saw the taxi driving away and my mother's tearstained face.

"Forgive me Mammy. Forgive me."

I saw her on her deathbed fighting for breath. She smiled at me and told me that she loved me.

"There is nothing to forgive. You had to go. I'm sorry that I never understood you."

I saw my unborn baby being taken away from me in a plastic bag. Fionn waved at me. He was fifteen. He blew me a kiss and I saw him standing tall and strong and he looked so like his dad. I wept for his death and promised that I would honour him. He asked me to light a candle for him to acknowledge his existence.

I saw my baby daughter being wrenched from my body by cold steel forceps and heard myself screaming out in agony. I took my young hand and embraced all the pain. I saw my ex-husband standing there and I told him goodbye. I saw our wedding day. It was so beautiful and we smiled at each other with such love in our eyes. I said goodbye to all the years we had had together. I wept and wept and wept.

I sat in the healing room and the tears of all the participants resonated in the sacred space.

"I told you that I wouldn't leave anybody behind," Thomas said. We all had faced our worst demons, preventing us from moving on and had come back to continue on another path in our lives. We had been guided by him to face our worst fears and he led us back to safety. Emer's gentle strength assisted us on this journey. She was always present throughout my personal struggles.

I had experienced the most remarkable event of my life. Every detail of my past had come back to me. Details that I had not wanted to remember. Smells that I had not wanted to smell. Words that I had not wanted to hear. Sights that I had not wanted to see. But that wonderful light in the tunnel had guided me through it all.

I went out into the forest during lunch break and smelled the trees for the first time in a long, long time. I touched the soft branches and drank in the sights around me. Everything seemed to be bluer and greener. The soft soil under my feet felt like brown spongy marshmallows. I was mesmerised by the intensity of everything that surrounded me. I could see the beauty around me for the first time. I could smell without fear. The forest seemed to embrace me and the wind tickled my face and hands. I felt totally at one with everything. I was dumbfounded.

Thomas was in the lobby. I asked him whether he'd mind if I embraced him. He was the first man I would embrace with openness and purity. It touched me greatly.

"Niamh, we have all been through great pain. That is our path. The warrior's path."

"That was tough," I sobbed, tears of relief streaming down my face. "I hit a mental wall later on and panicked when those painful memories came flooding back in technicolour."

"We knew we were dealing with a nine-year-old," Thomas and Emer said.

I had closed myself off emotionally after my traumatic childhood. I had never developed emotionally into a woman. I was stuck in a bubble of fear and powerlessness. All the abuse that had taken place was because I had not the tools to empower myself. My soul had been retrieved and given back to me. I could move forward as an empowered woman, having released all the pain of the past.

Forty-three years of self-loathing. Forty-three years of trying to be somebody else. Now I had released all that blocked my path. I could now honour the person who I was. The person I am. Nobody can take that power away. I felt giddy and exhausted at the same time. I had retrieved my very soul. My very being.

At the end of the weekend we all had to take part in a final fire ceremony. Here we had to release our past and grieve and honour it. By throwing our small articles into the fire, it would enable us to move forward. One by one, we greeted the fire and threw our past into her fury. I threw a black-and-white photo of Mammy and Daddy into the red flames, a wedding photo of Lucas and I, and a photo of me as a young woman looking shyly into the lens. They all met the fury of the fire and my tears kept on rolling down my cheeks. I was letting go of all that was preventing me from moving on. We all cried softly as the flames became higher and higher and each participant stepped forward to release their anchors from their past.

The fire blazed. The sound of the Shamanic drum beckoned me to the flames. I felt that I was in another lifetime. I felt like a warrior grieving for her lost companions. I sang a song that was in another language, yet familiar and that emerged like a geyser from deep in my belly. I don't know where it came from. It was a song filled with grief and sorrow. It echoed through the forest and as each person threw their past life into the red fury, I howled for all that was gone forever. I sang this strange haunting melody, but I knew it was an integral part of me. It sang with the beat of the drums. It was my warrior's song of long ago.

"Niamh, that was remarkable. I felt every note that you sang. It was like an old Indian squaw singing her grief," Turlough said to me. He, amazingly stood tall and straight. His own healing had taken place. I knew his heart was strong again.

"Turlough, I release you for being responsible for me. I can take care of myself now," I said tearfully.

"Oh, Niamh, I only ever wanted you to be happy," Turlough blurted out.

"No, Turlough, that was never your responsibility. We'll now embrace as equals, not little sister and big brother," I replied.

We hugged and I knew that our relationship was changed forever. I said farewell to his fatherly embrace and welcomed our new love for each other.

We all had tears in our eyes and when the last piece of our past was engulfed in the flames, the fire miraculously died. It was an unbelievable sight. We all stood there in awe of the holy flames that accepted our pain.

I know now that this is my healing song. It is the song I have sought for all those years of cruelty and abuse.

I had sung right from my babyhood into adulthood. This song was a confirmation of all those songs. It was a tribute to having survived those events. I used it as a place in which to honour my pain. The song is engrained in my soul. It is my song. Nobody can take it away from me. It will continue on its journey with me, purely and safely.

Thomas and Emer were spot on. I had closed myself off from growing up since that dreadful day in the dark oak wardrobe. Emotionally, I had stood still all those years. Forty-three years of struggling was over now. I knew that. I had come through. It wouldn't be easy, I acknowledged. But hell, my previous path was not easy either. I was exhausted but elated.

I left Aberdeen and the sound of the Shamanic drums kept rhythm to my beating heart. They echoed in the valley and I took them with me. I saw the purple heather out of the car window. A startling smell of mossy heather invaded all my senses. It took my breath away. I hadn't had that recollection in such a long, long time.

The airport was a kaleidoscope of colours and noise. Everything was in stereo. The noise was unbelievable to my ears and the colours blinding to my eyes. I felt dizzy with the intensity of my senses.

I went up to a little bar in the departures hall.

"Could I have an orange juice please?" I asked the young barman. He looked about eighteen. His hair was gelled and ruffled in the current fashion.

He stared at me.

"Did anyone ever tell you that you have the most beautiful eyes?" he said.

I don't know who was more startled, him or me.

"Thank you so much for the compliment," I beamed. I smiled and felt that sunshine had exploded throughout my body. I felt a tingling sensation and burst out laughing.

The barman joined in and the young girl assisting him thought we were mad.

"I just had this incredible urge to tell you," he said. He blushed and started to turn away, before changing his mind and handing me a free juice.

"Your journey has just started," he said very matter-of-factly, in a deep manly voice.

He waved me off and I felt as if something outside of our control was taking place. Yet it didn't frighten me. On the contrary, it felt comfortable and familiar. I couldn't explain the feeling because I didn't know it myself.

I hurried away and my lilac ankle boots clicked down the tiled departure hall. I wanted them to be silent because I felt everybody was staring at me. My head was spinning with all the new feelings and sensations flooding into my body.

Customs waved me through whilst most of the other passengers were stripped of all their bits and pieces.

An elderly woman approached me.

"Have a safe flight," she said. "Everything will be all right. Follow your heart." She disappeared into the crowd.

On the plane the stewardess came over four times to ask if everything was okay. I thought there was something radically wrong with me. Did I look sick? Did I have some sort of weird attraction for people after my special weekend? My weekend. My wonderful, amazing weekend.

Oisin stood at the door to greet me. She looked tall and elegant. Her long legs were awkward and coltish. Her beautiful smile wasinnocent and open.

"Sweetheart, I only brought myself home this time,"

I said. "I didn't have time to buy a present." I always inundated her with presents when I was away.

"But Mom, do you not realise that you were always enough?" she replied. "You are enough." She handed me a CD of Susan Boyle's *I Dreamed a Dream.*

We embraced and I inhaled her trendy perfume and touched her long golden hair. It felt as if I was touching her for the first time. I had no fear.

"Mammy, steady on there. You'll squeeze the living daylights out of me," she said.

Reluctantly I let her go. Mozart was waiting for his cuddles. I swept him up in my arms and his doggy smell permeated all my senses. I cried and cried. He licked my face. I felt his pink wet tongue on my tearstained cheek. It felt warm and rough. It tickled me. The sensation was new to me. I began to laugh hysterically. Mozart barked and jumped out of my arms, my outburst a bit too sudden for him. He sniffed my hand as if to confirm that it really was me.

"You look different," Oisin said. "You look … what's the word ... lighter. Yeah, Mammy, lighter."

Oisin was right. I felt as if I was springing through the room. I not only felt year's younger, but also looked years younger. I caught a glimpse of myself in our tall oriental mirror in the living room. I saw a reflection gazing back at me. It was familiar, yet not. A younger blonde woman glanced back at me. She was voluptuous and sexy and happy. Her skin was radiant and her eyes twinkled like her father's used to. A word came into her mind. This time a word that meant something. Happy. Plain and simple. She was happy. I blew her a kiss and she winked back at me. She swayed through the room and felt like one hot smokin' mama. She felt. She had feelings. They were indescribable.

I touched the cold glass of water and smelled the small pink roses in the dainty vase. My lovely daughter had bought them for me.

"Time for walkies in the forest. Time, Mozart to find our way."

I had this inexplicable urge to go to the local forest. I followed my gut feeling. No questions. No reasoning. No doubts.

The wind swept through my long hair and I followed the thick overgrown path. My spirit guide had told me to find the forked tree. I walked with Mozart at my side. The wind beckoned me to go on. The sun shone intermittently through the trees and I did not falter. I felt the power of my spirit guide pushing me forward.

It started to rain and the drops bounced off the rocky path. I saw a woman in the distance. She was pointing to a tree. Something moved way up high. Other people had gathered around to see what it was. I was compelled to follow.

My power animal was perched high and proud between the forked branches. He was sitting waiting for me. I gazed at him and he blinked and acknowledged me. He suddenly took off in flight and soared high above me. He circled twice and flew away into the distance. Silence pierced the damp greenness. Nobody dared to say anything. They looked at my small canine friend and me.

I felt free. No, I *am* free. I had found the essence of who I am. The wind changed direction and seemed to celebrate with me. It surrounded me with its vibrant sounds. Tears of joy rolled down my cheeks.

These were special tears. I asked permission of the forked tree to spend some time with him. He gladly accepted my back against his sturdy old trunk. I took a small candle out of my pocket and lit it for my dead son Fionn, as promised. The small flame flickered in the afternoon sun. Now it was safe to acknowledge his existence. I sang my healing song. It ricocheted through the trees. It bellowed through my soul. Mozart joined in and howled in unison.

The people stopped and stared. I didn't care. I was home. I was me.

EPILOGUE

Oisin, Mozart and I have moved twice since the completion of this book. We have found peace and tranquility in an old Victorian apartment on the outskirts of The Hague. The list of dreams that I wrote as a young woman and then tore and scattered in my room like snowflakes are now coming true. I wished that I could write a book. And I have. I wished that I could sing with an orchestra. I have. Many more wishes are on my list. I know that I will achieve them. My final dream would be to help open up an Enlightenment Centre (for Thomas and Emer) to heal all those troubled people who need help and sanctuary and to release their abusive pasts. It will happen, if it's meant to happen. My warrior's path knows no fear.

Lucas and I are on speaking terms. We share the love of our daughter. I see him regularly at violin and singing concerts. I hope someday that we will be friends again.

CPSIA information can be obtained at www.ICGtesting.com
Printed in the USA
BVOW011146041212

307257BV00004B/10/P